GW01236824

MERRY CHRISTMAS

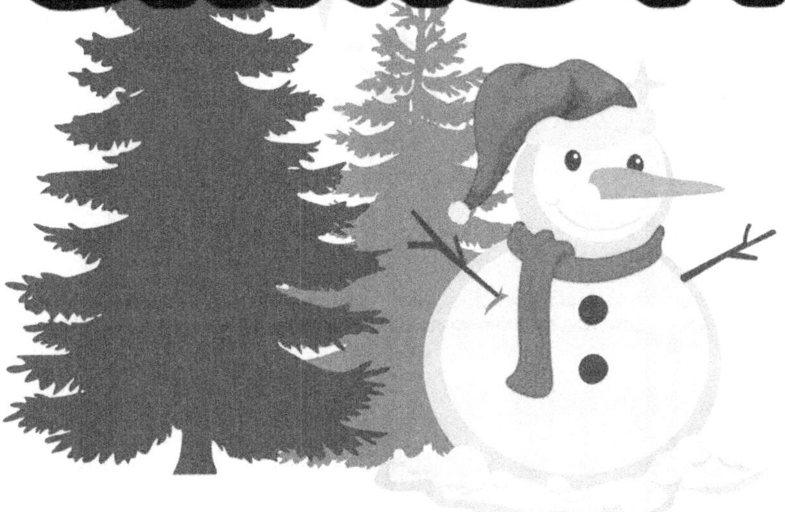

THIS BOOKBELONGS TO

____

____

COLOR TEST PAGE

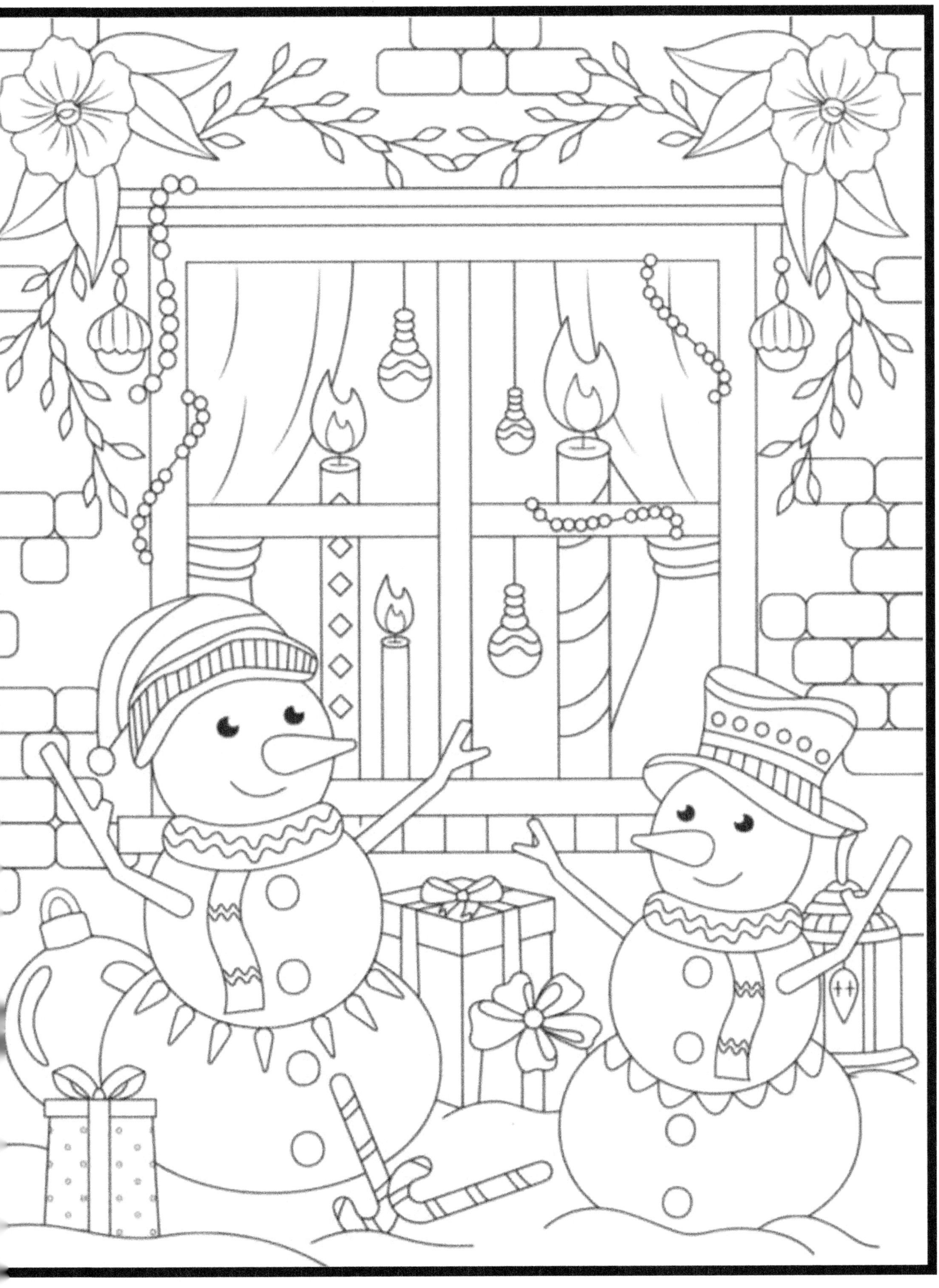

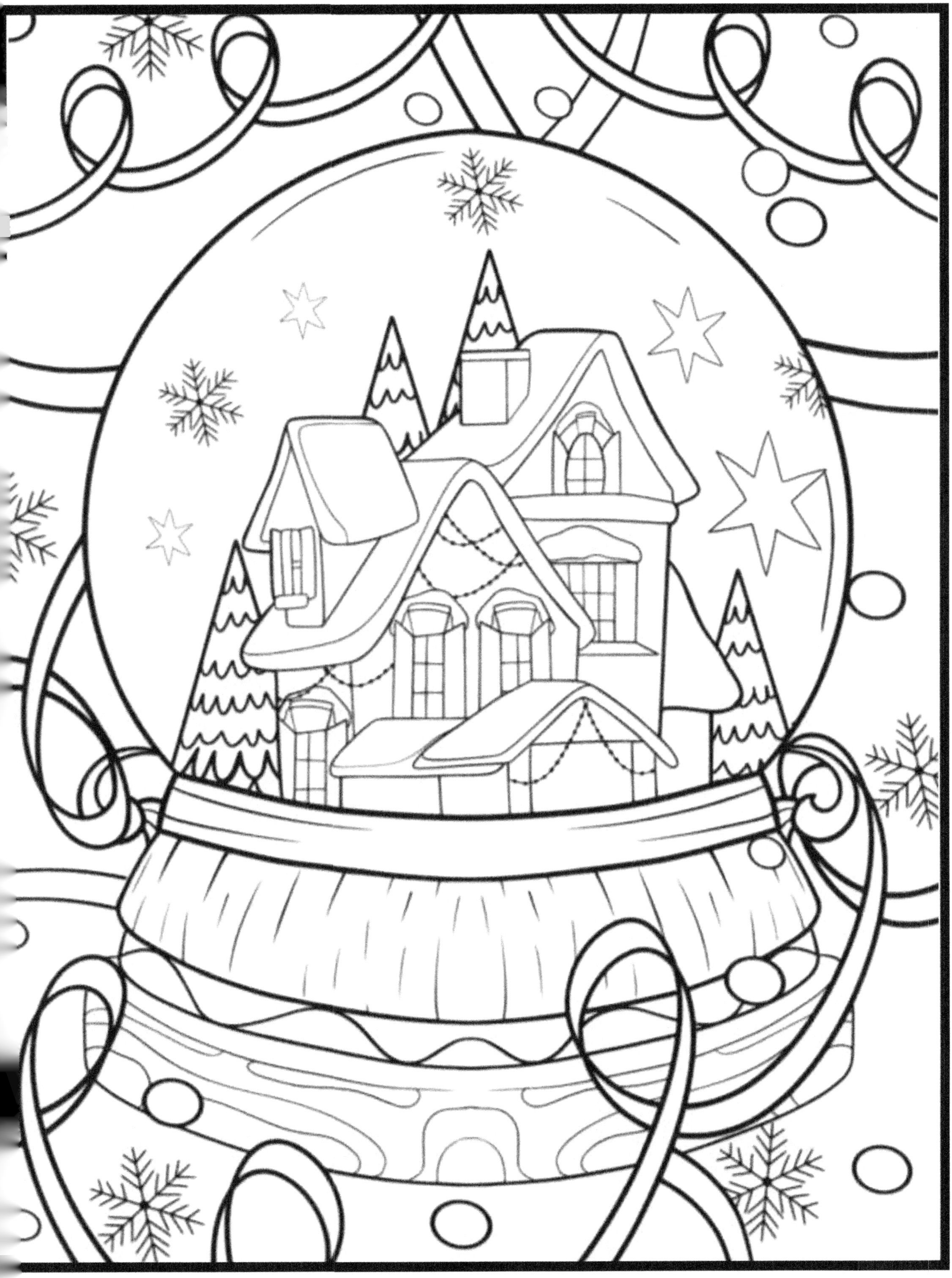

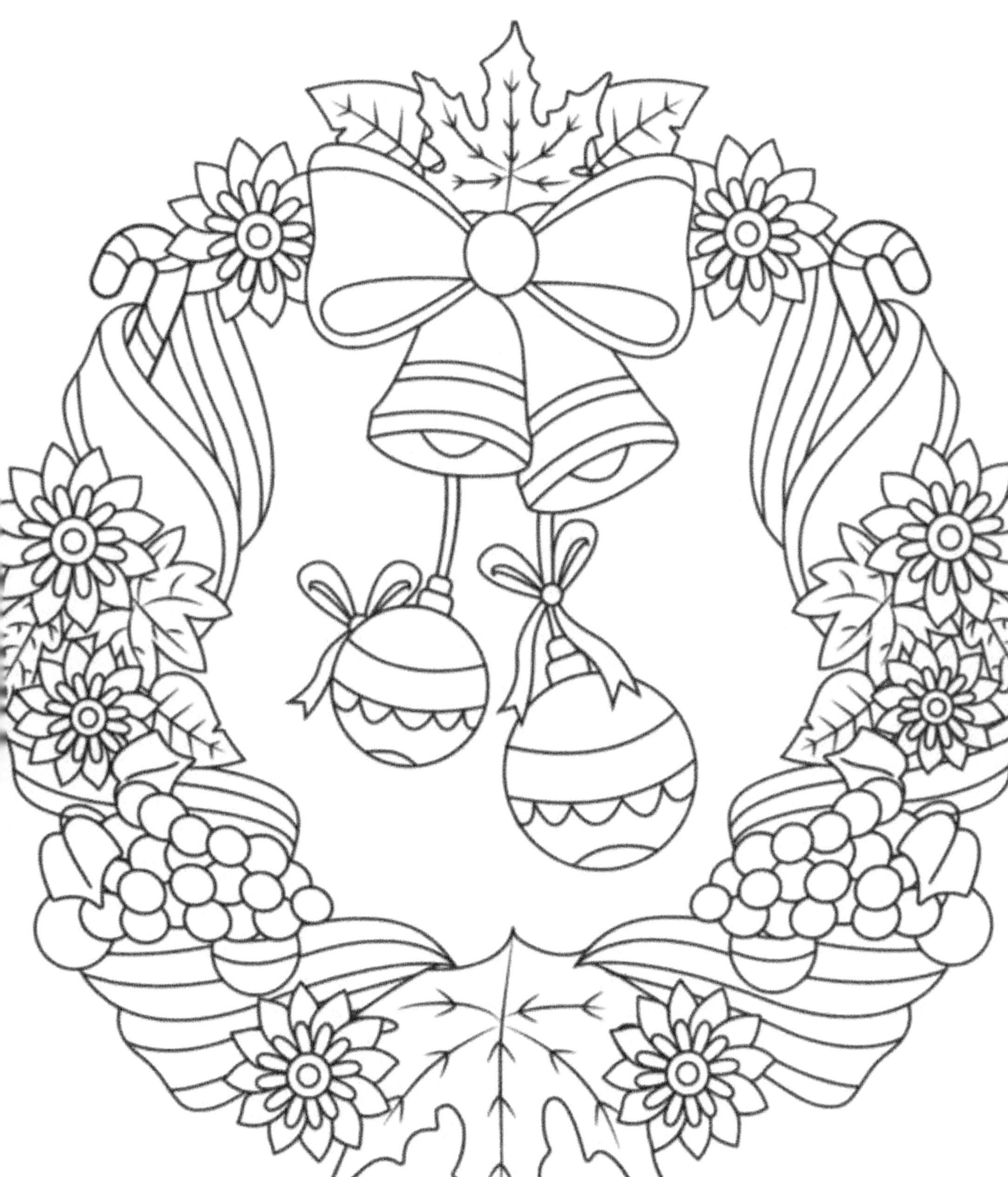

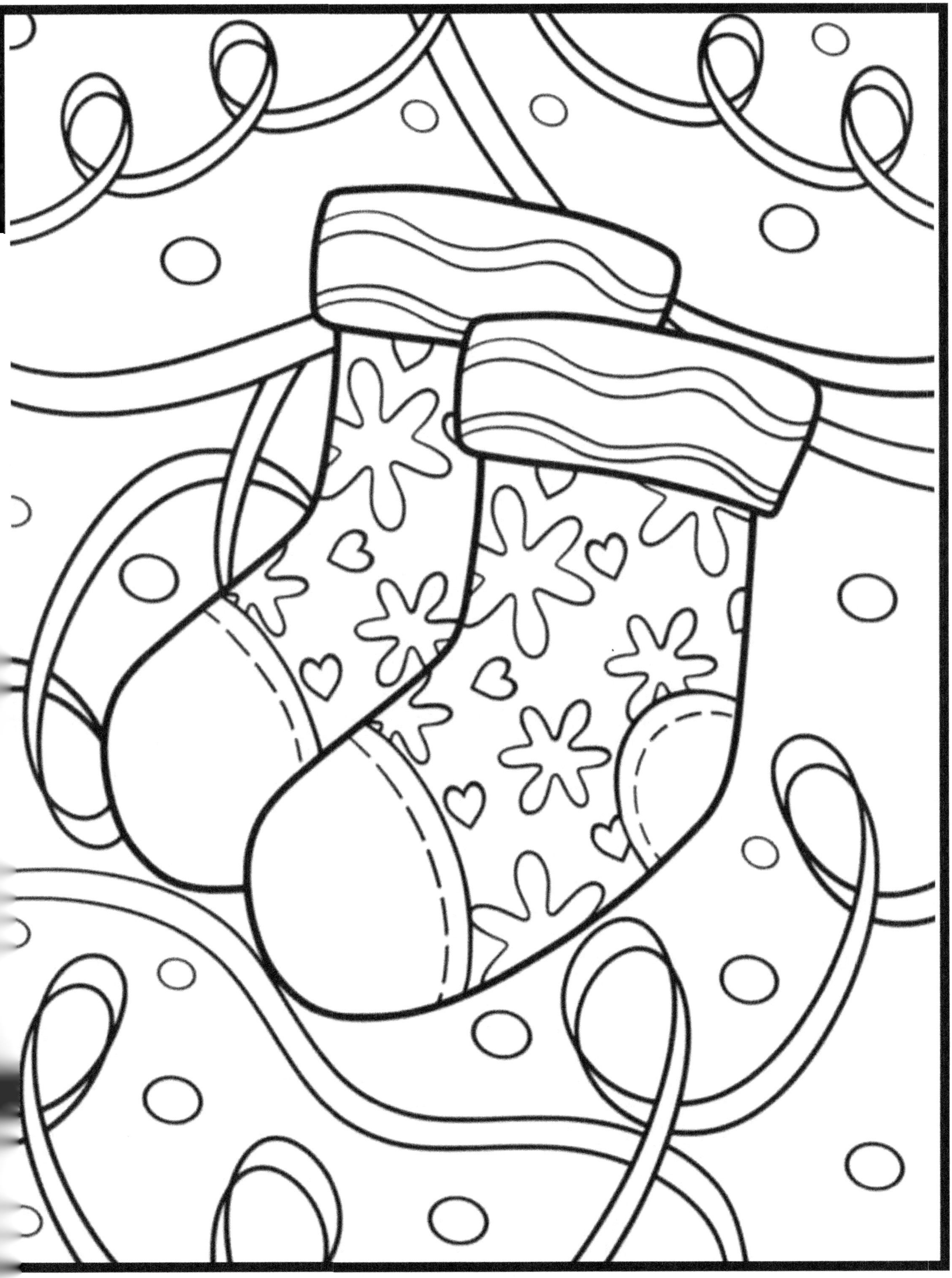

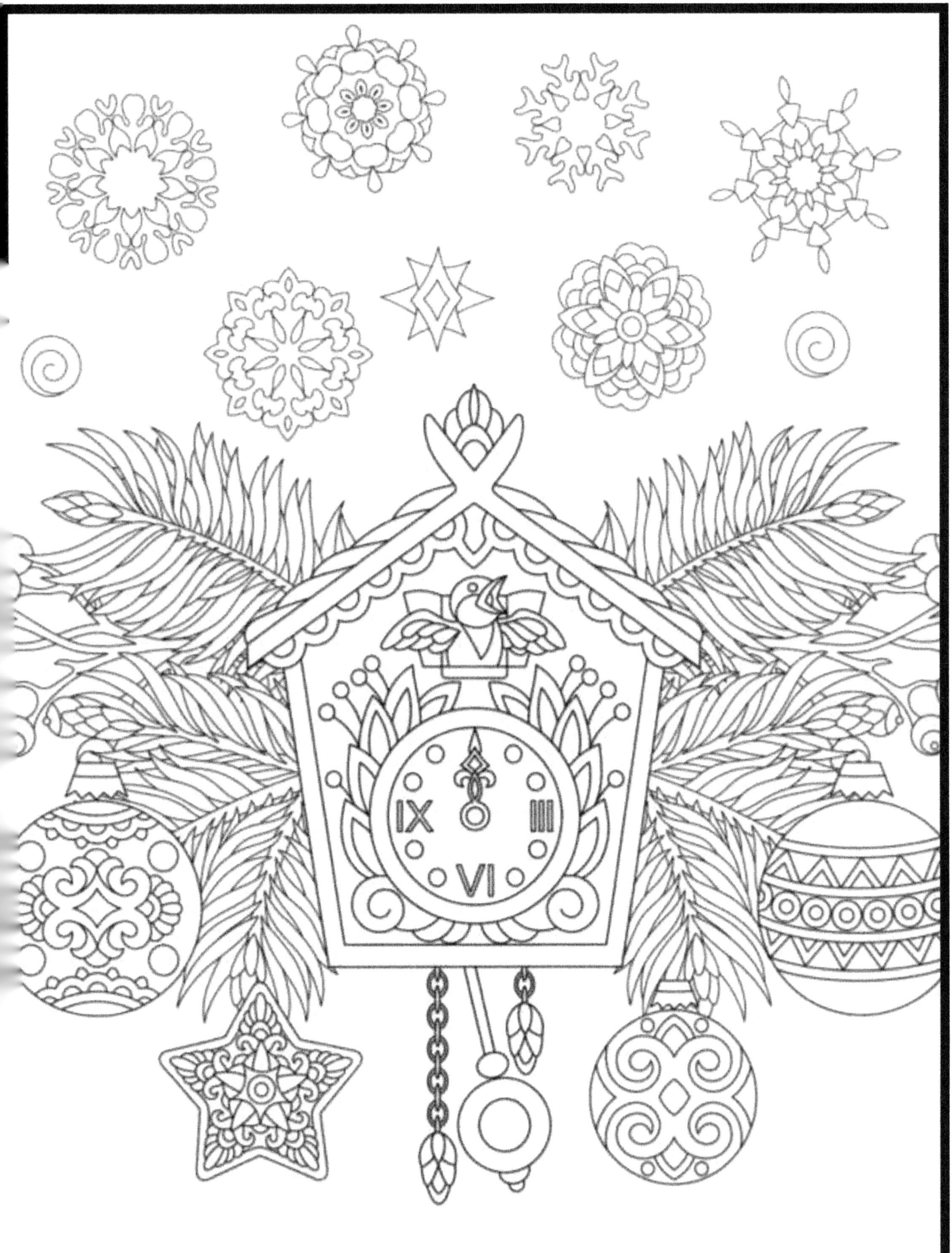
IX
III
VI

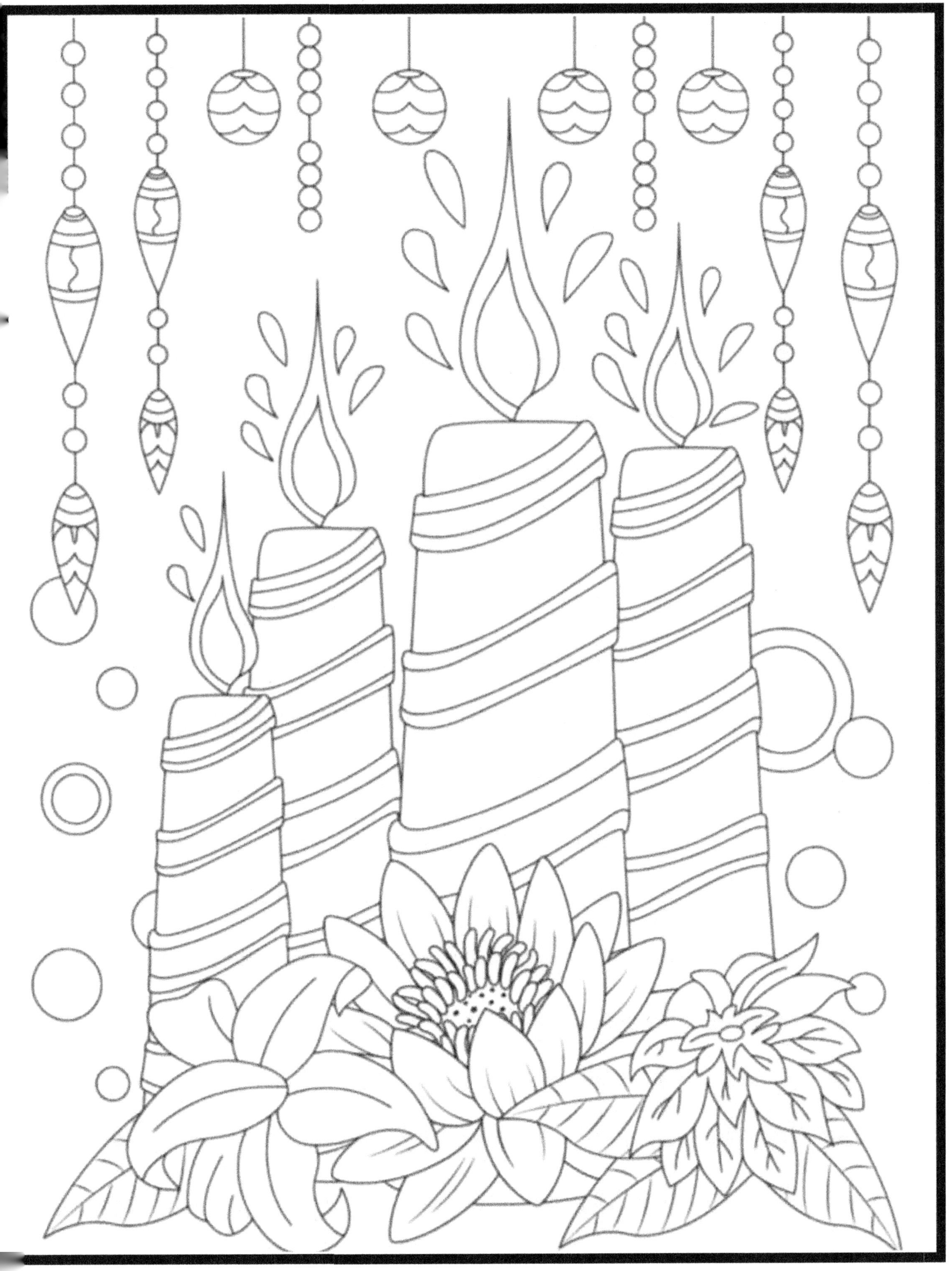

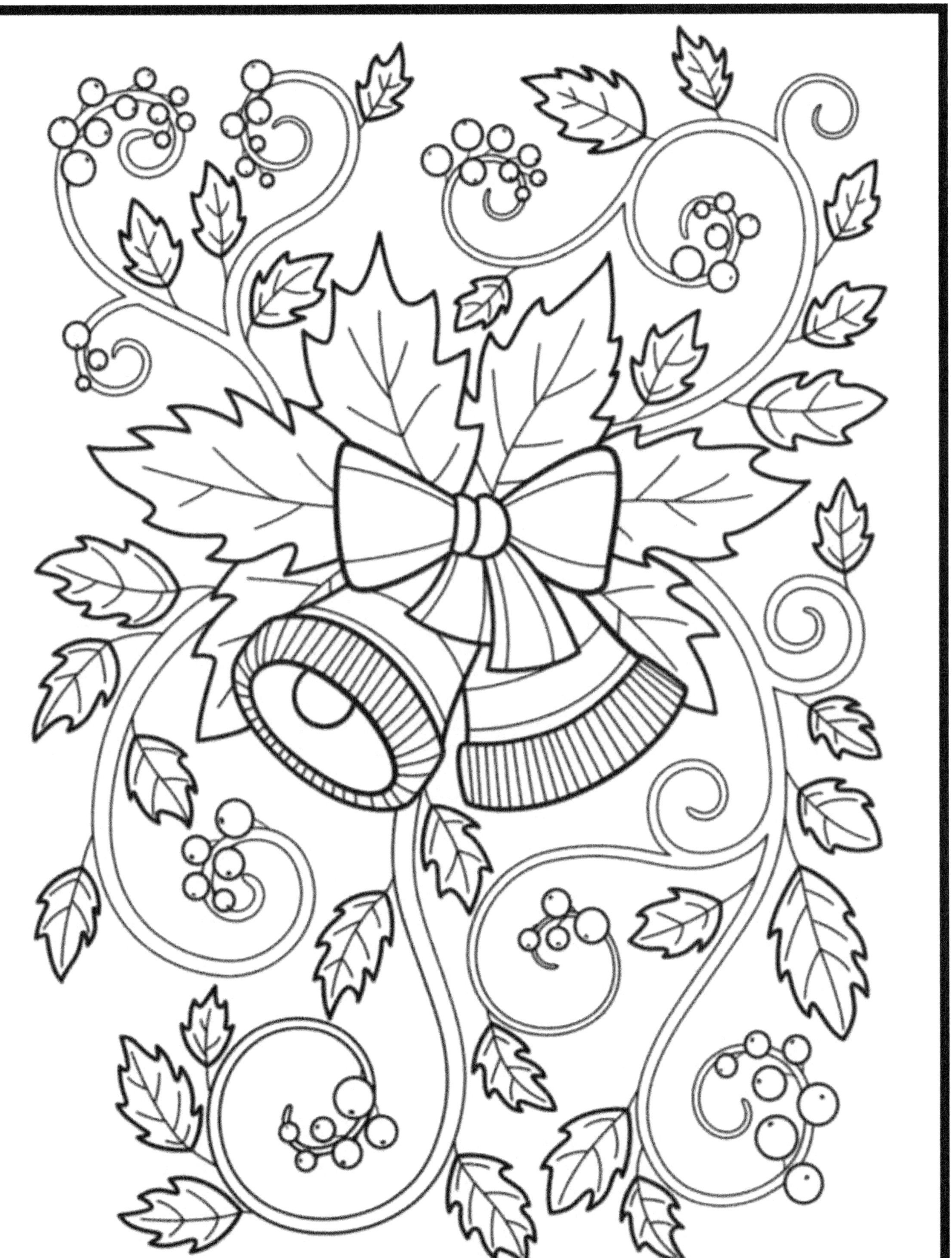

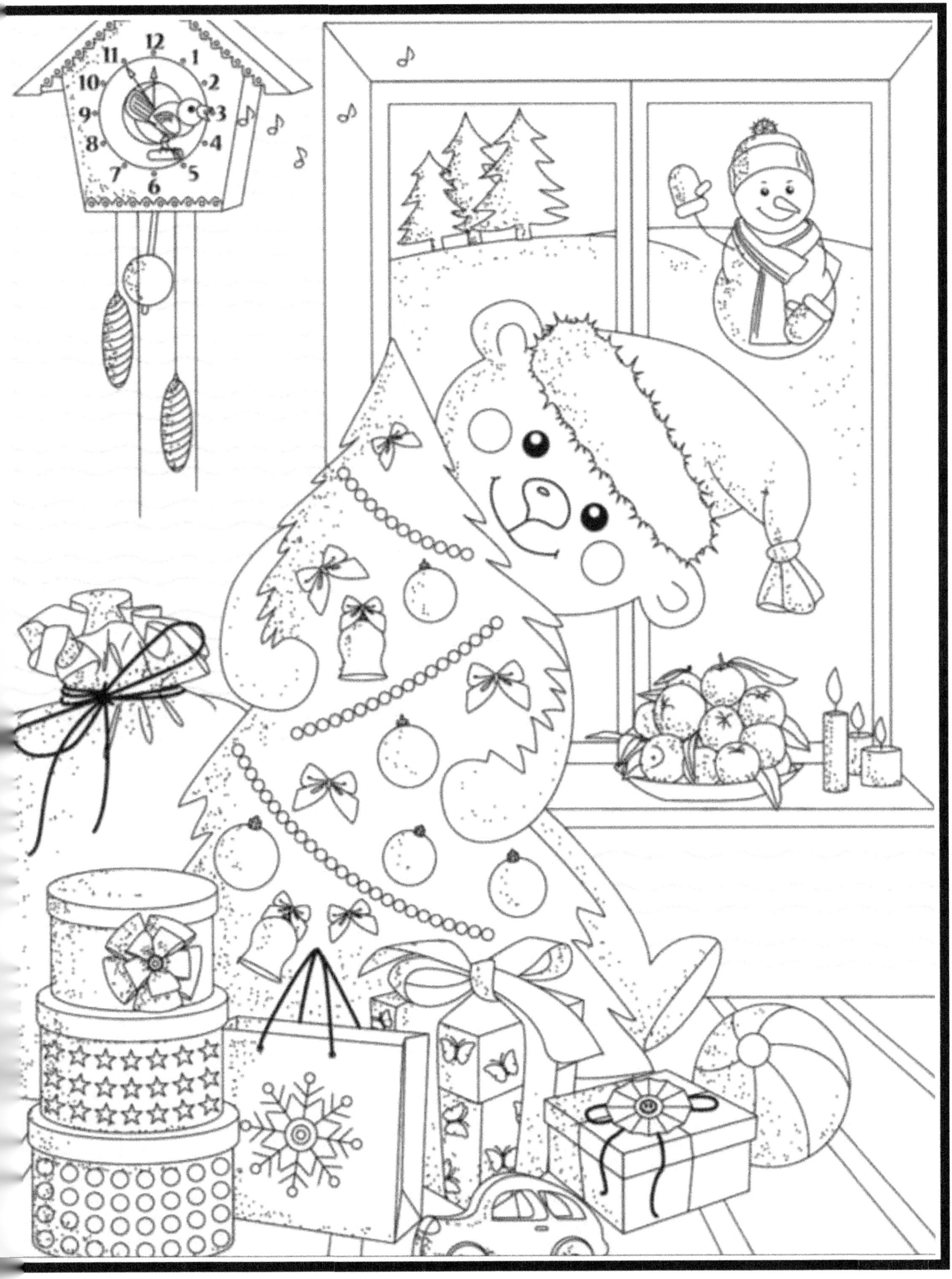
12
11
1
10
2
9
3
8
4
7
5
6

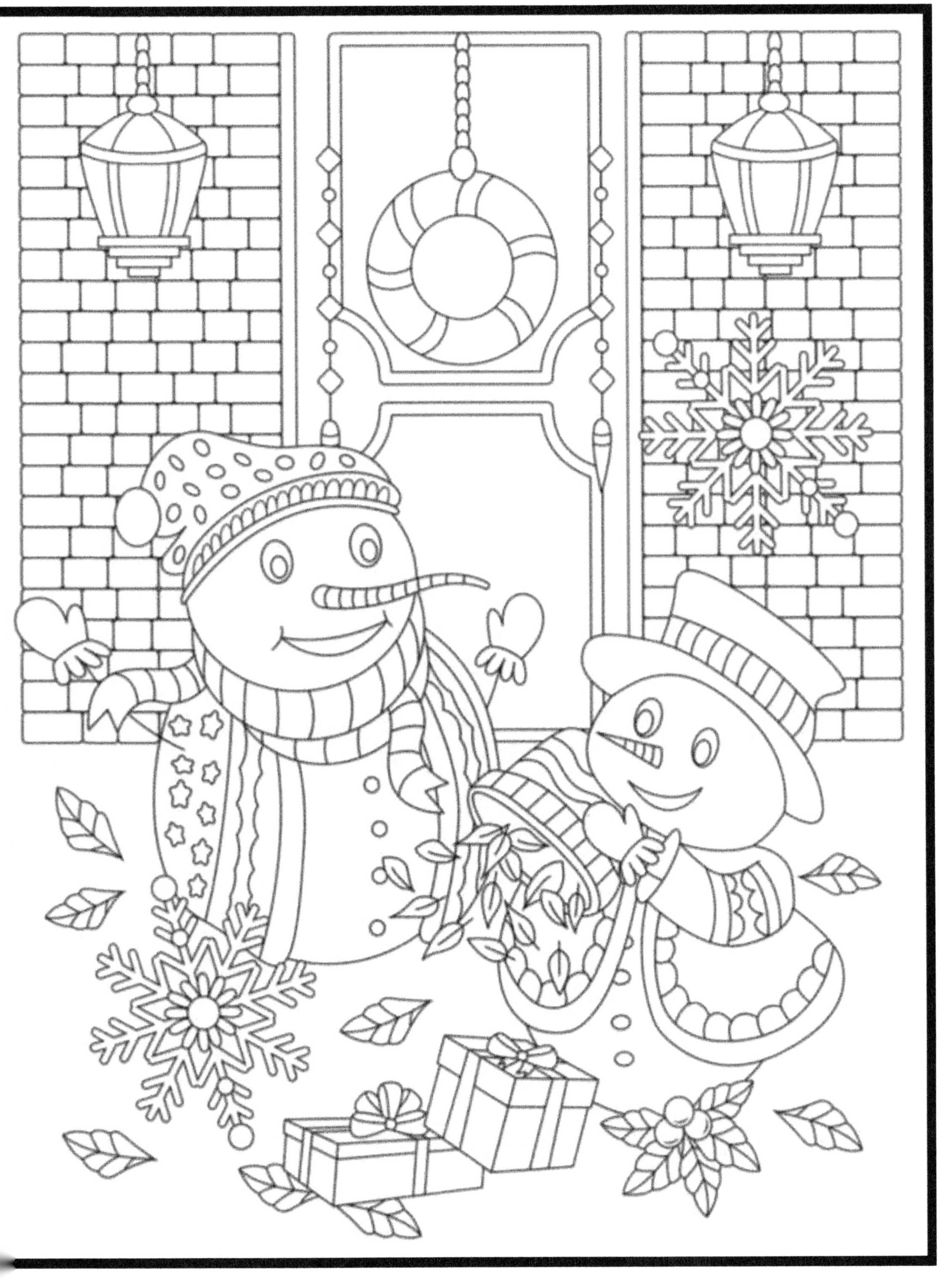

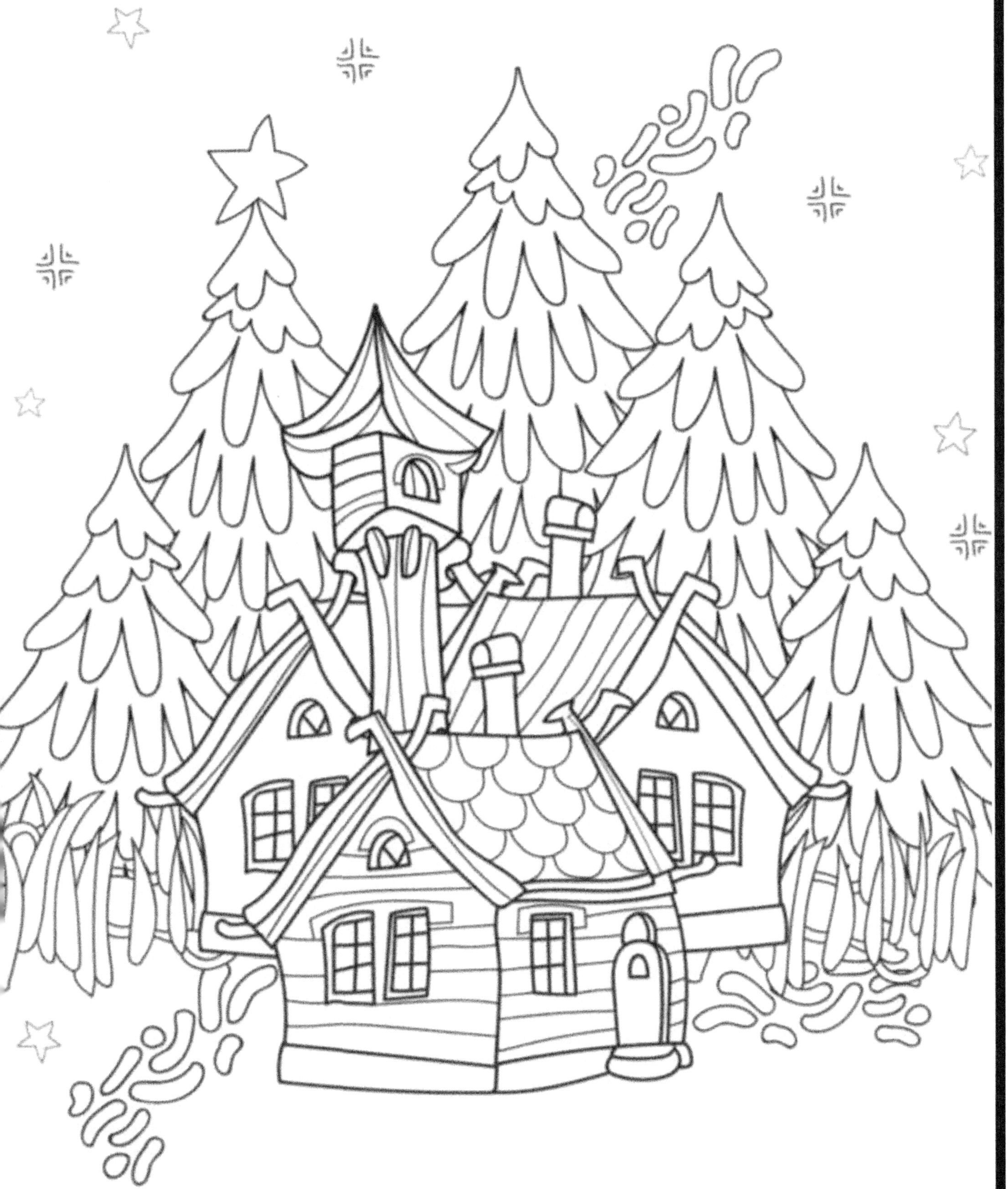

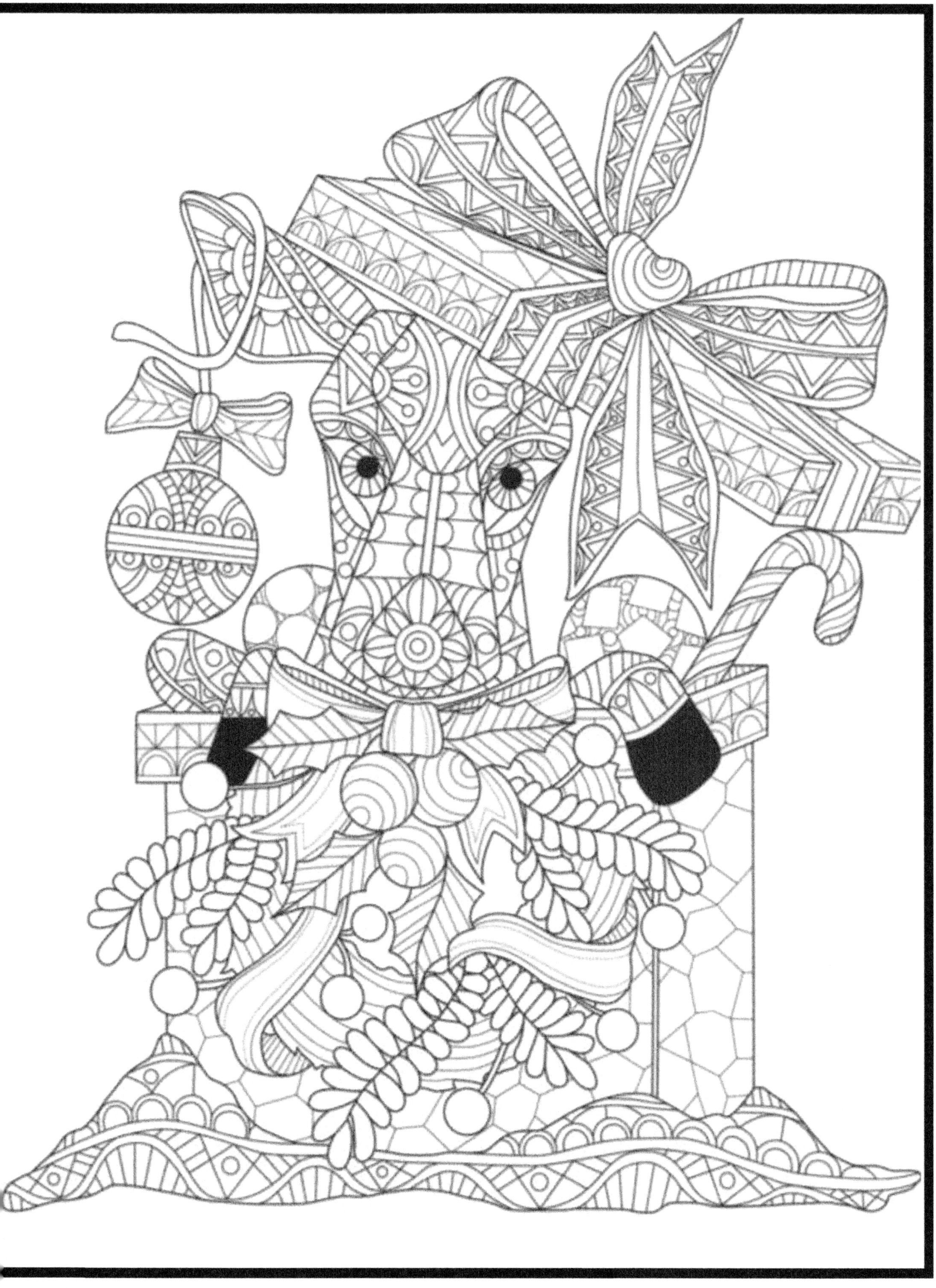

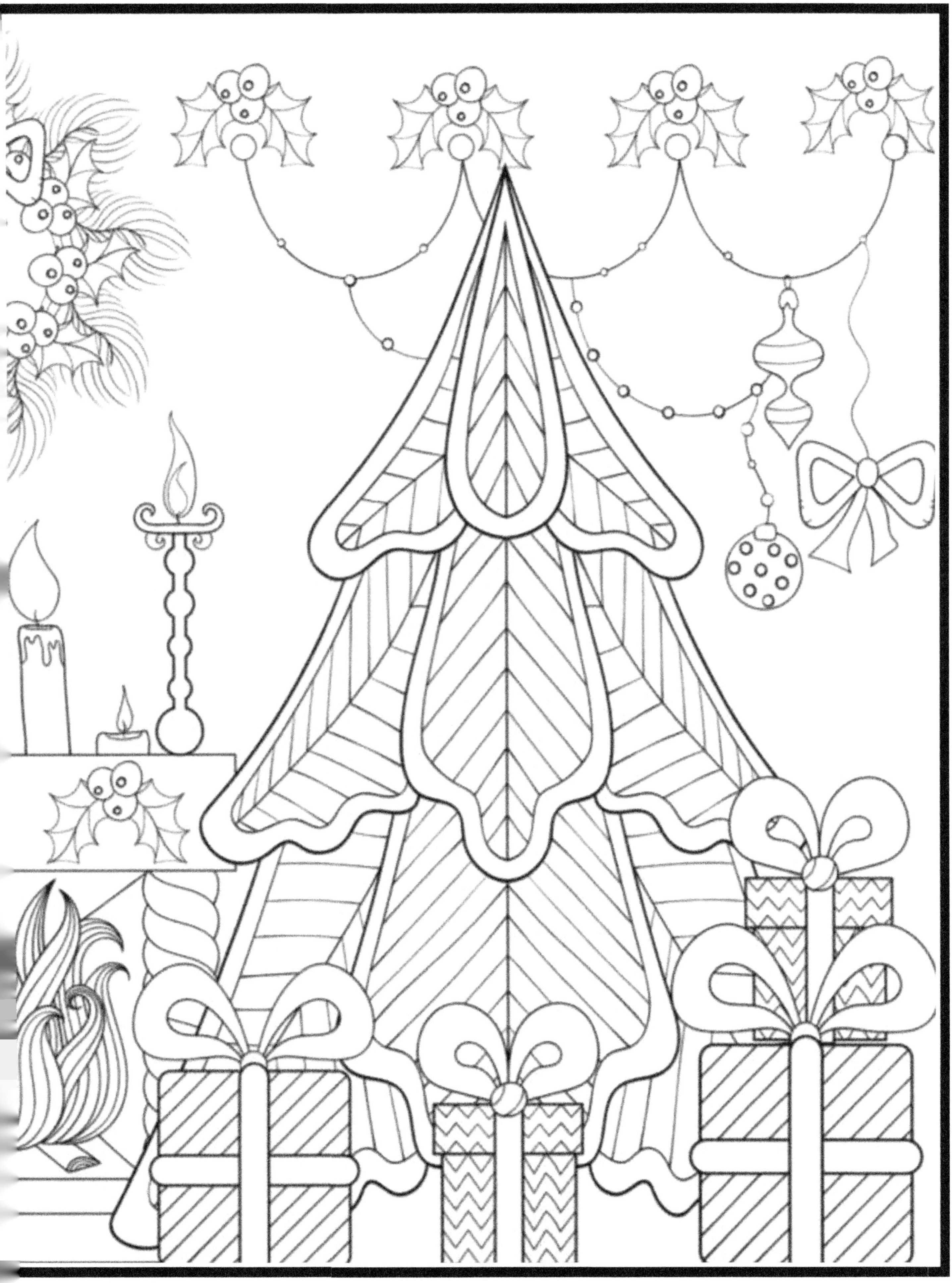

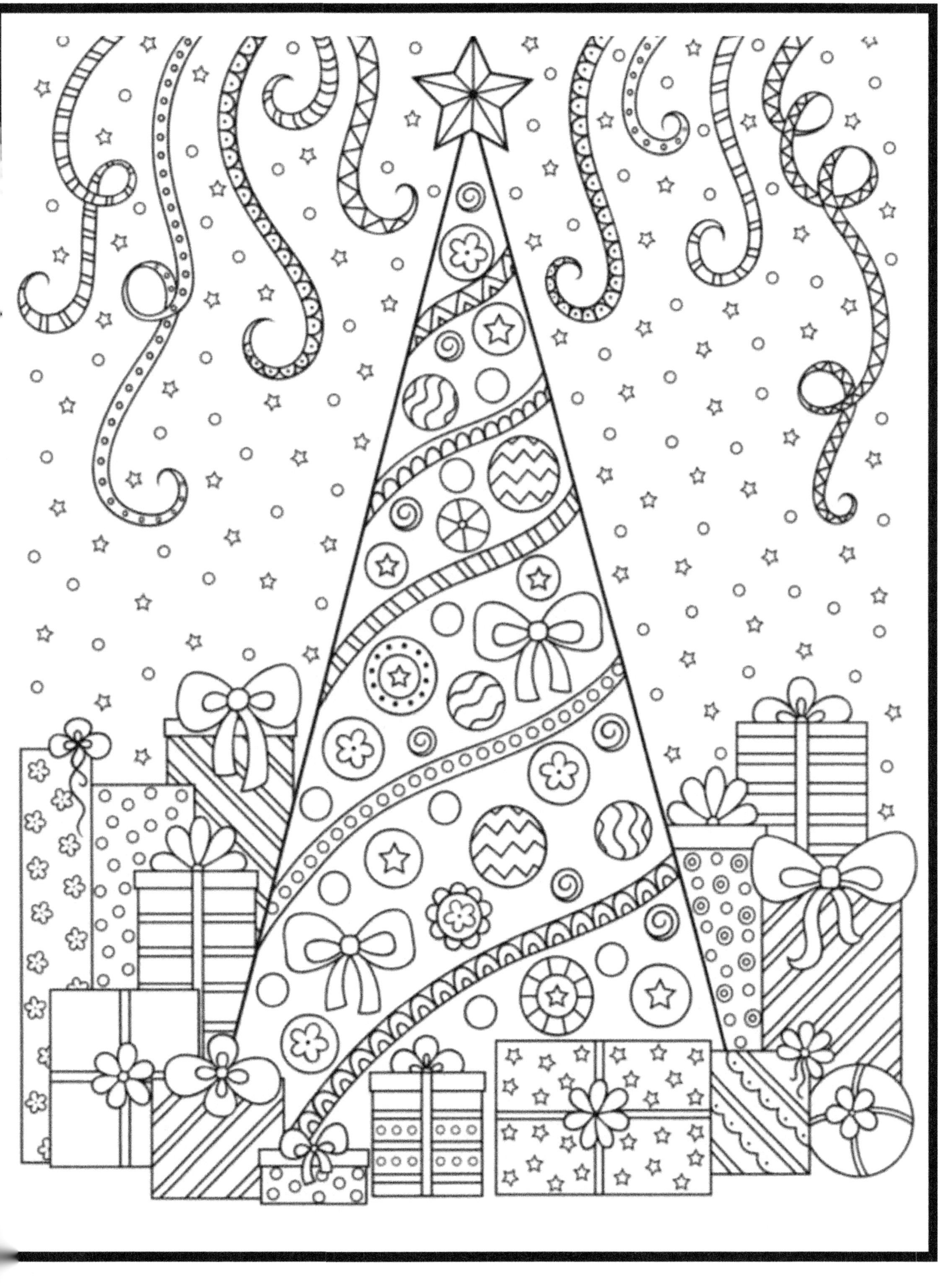

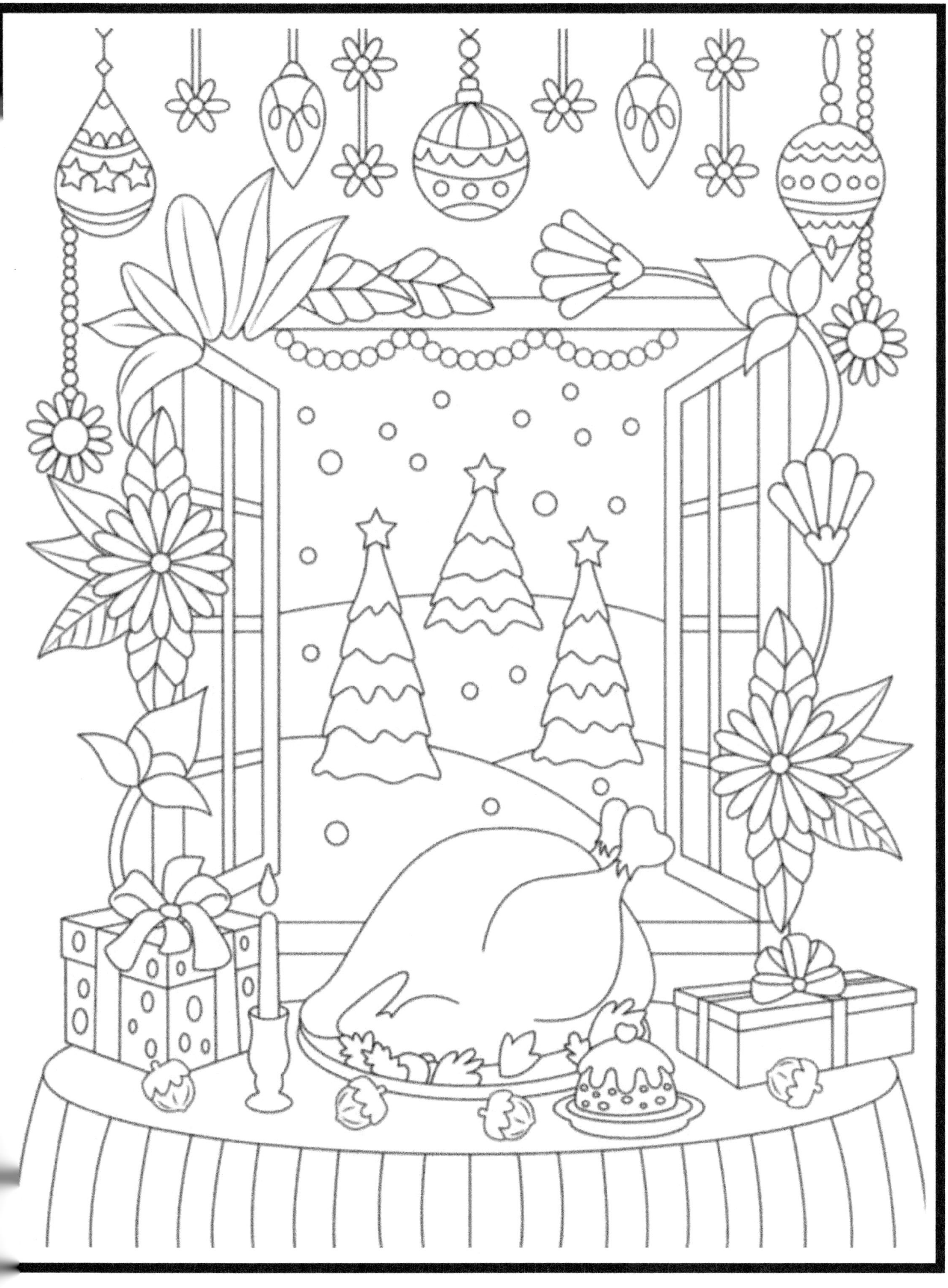

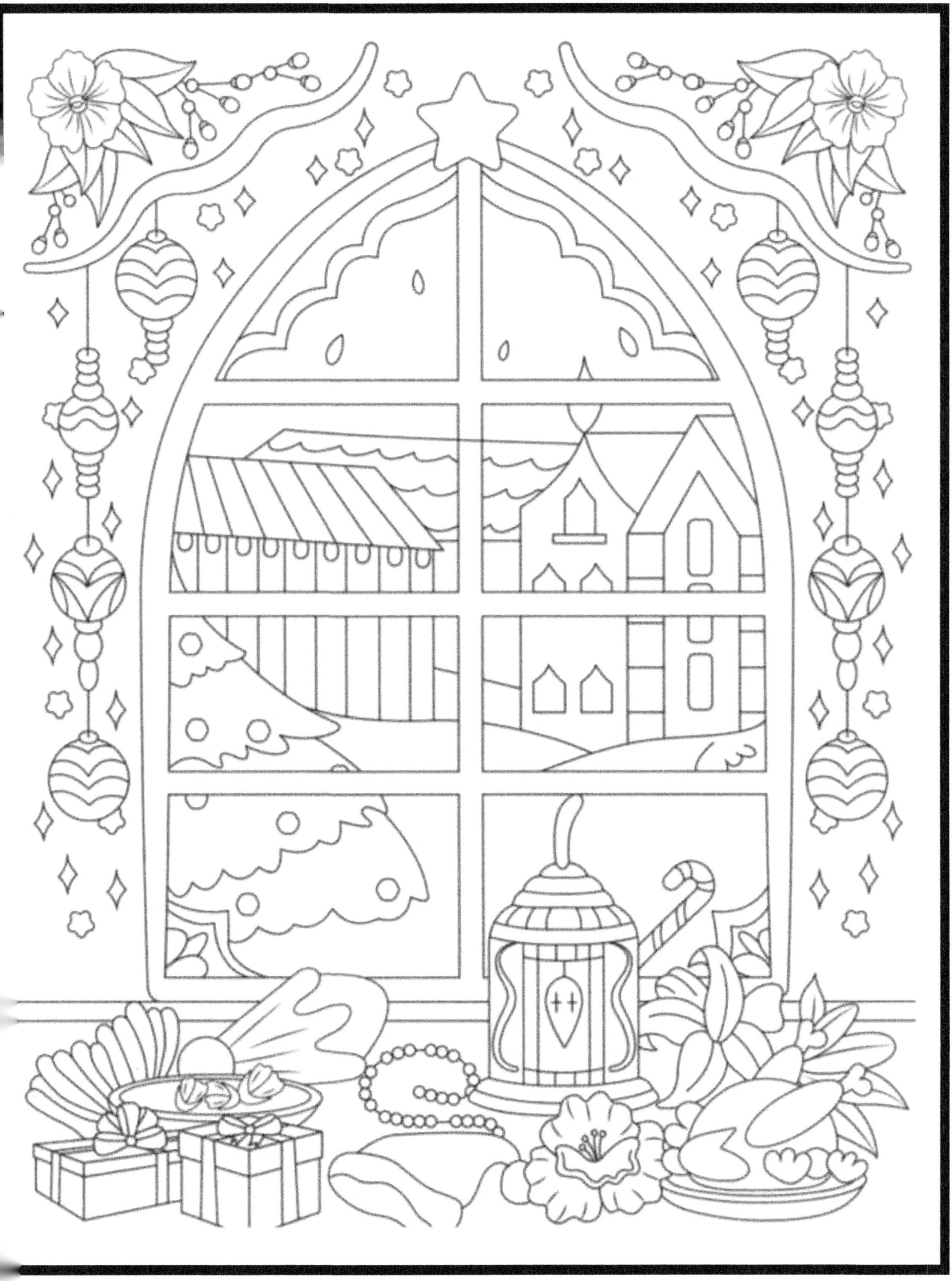

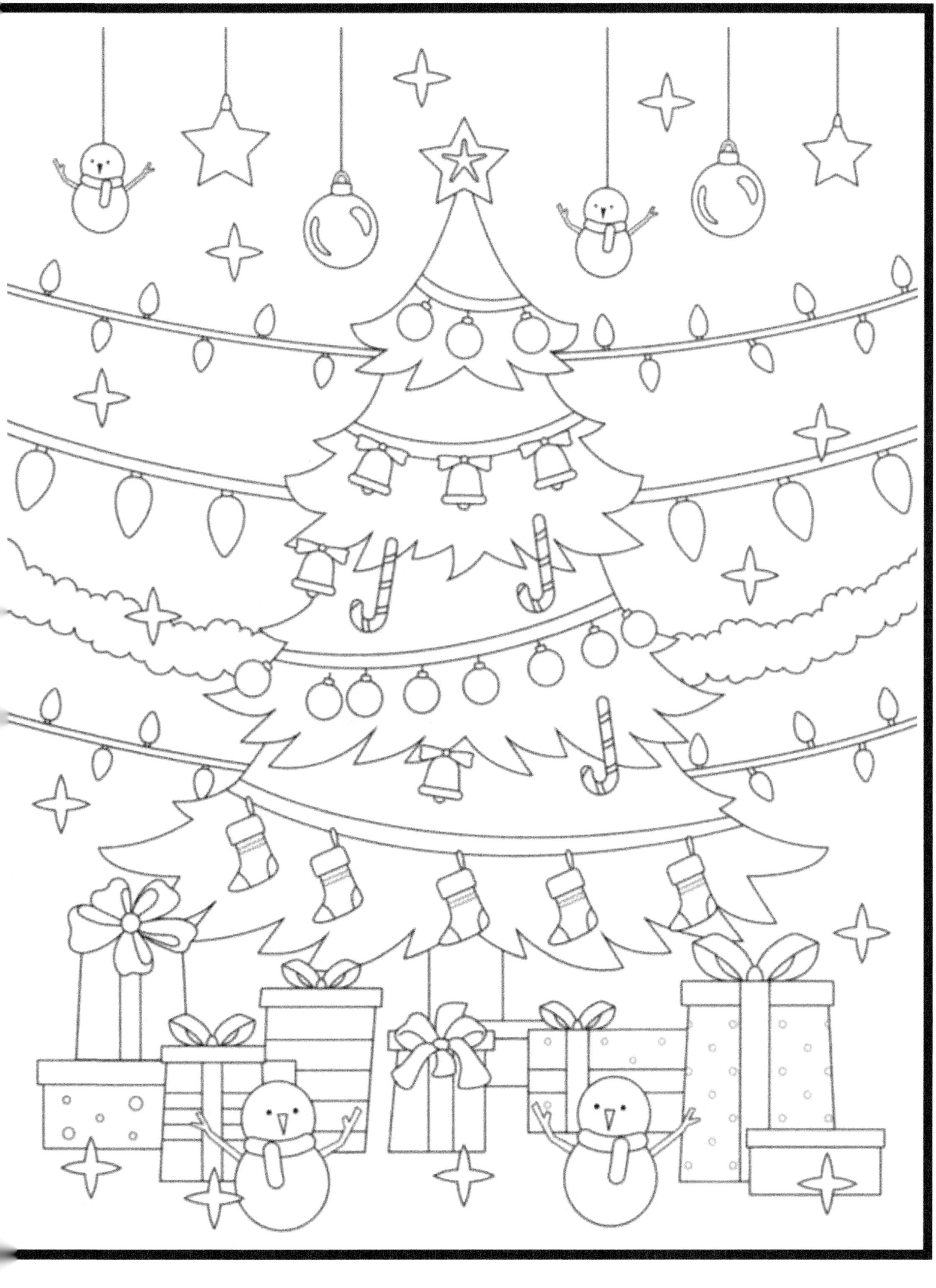

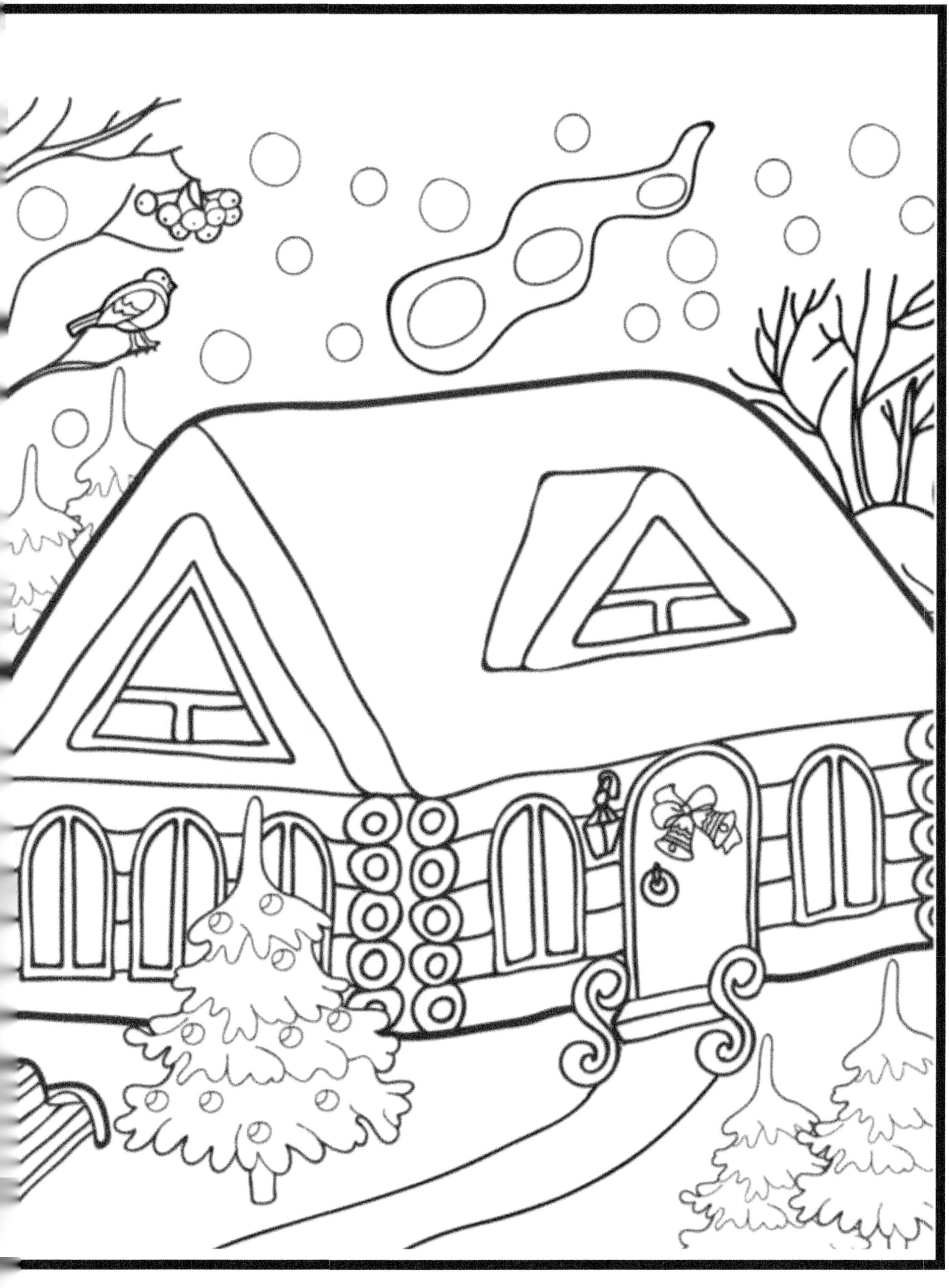

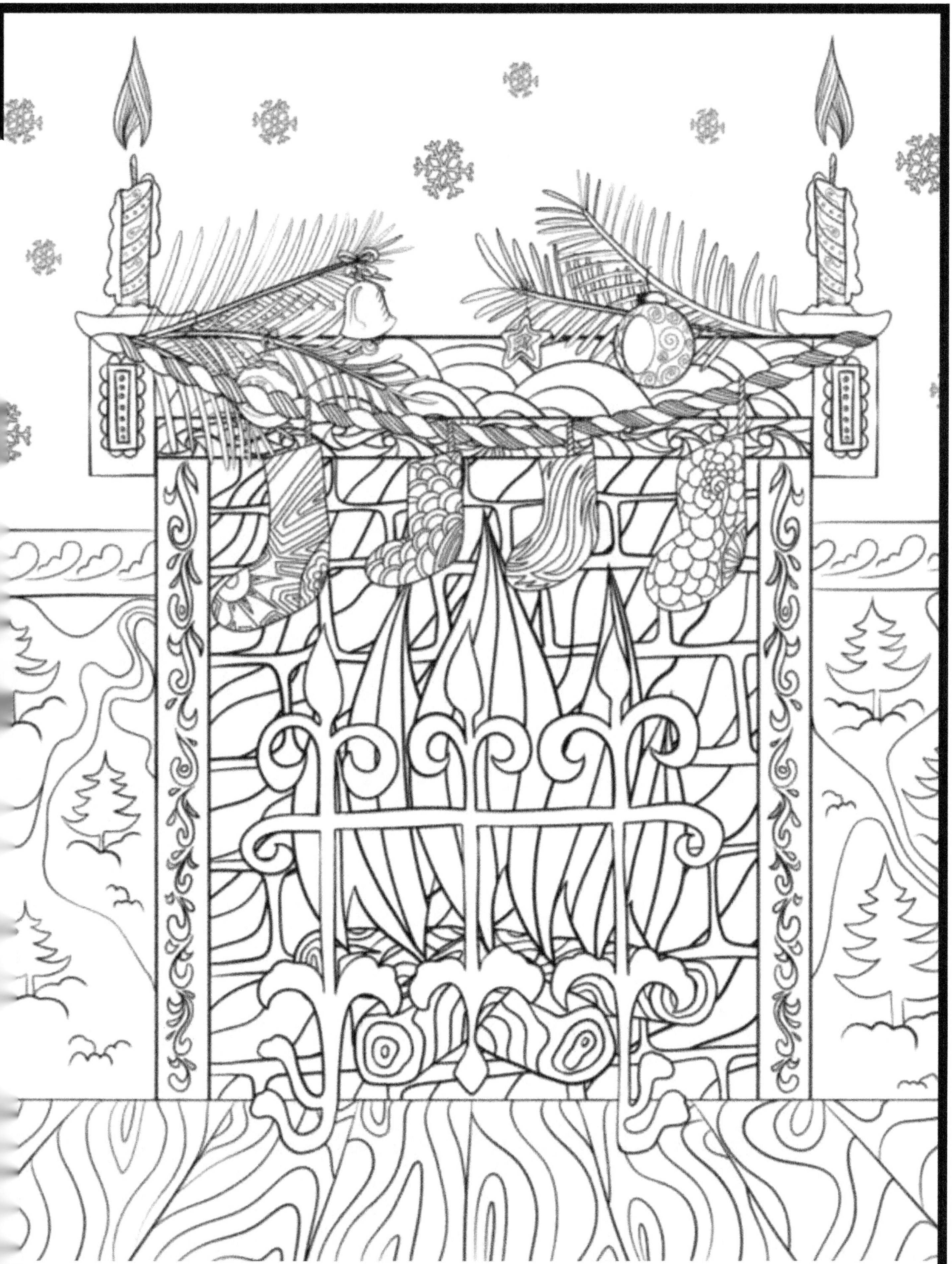

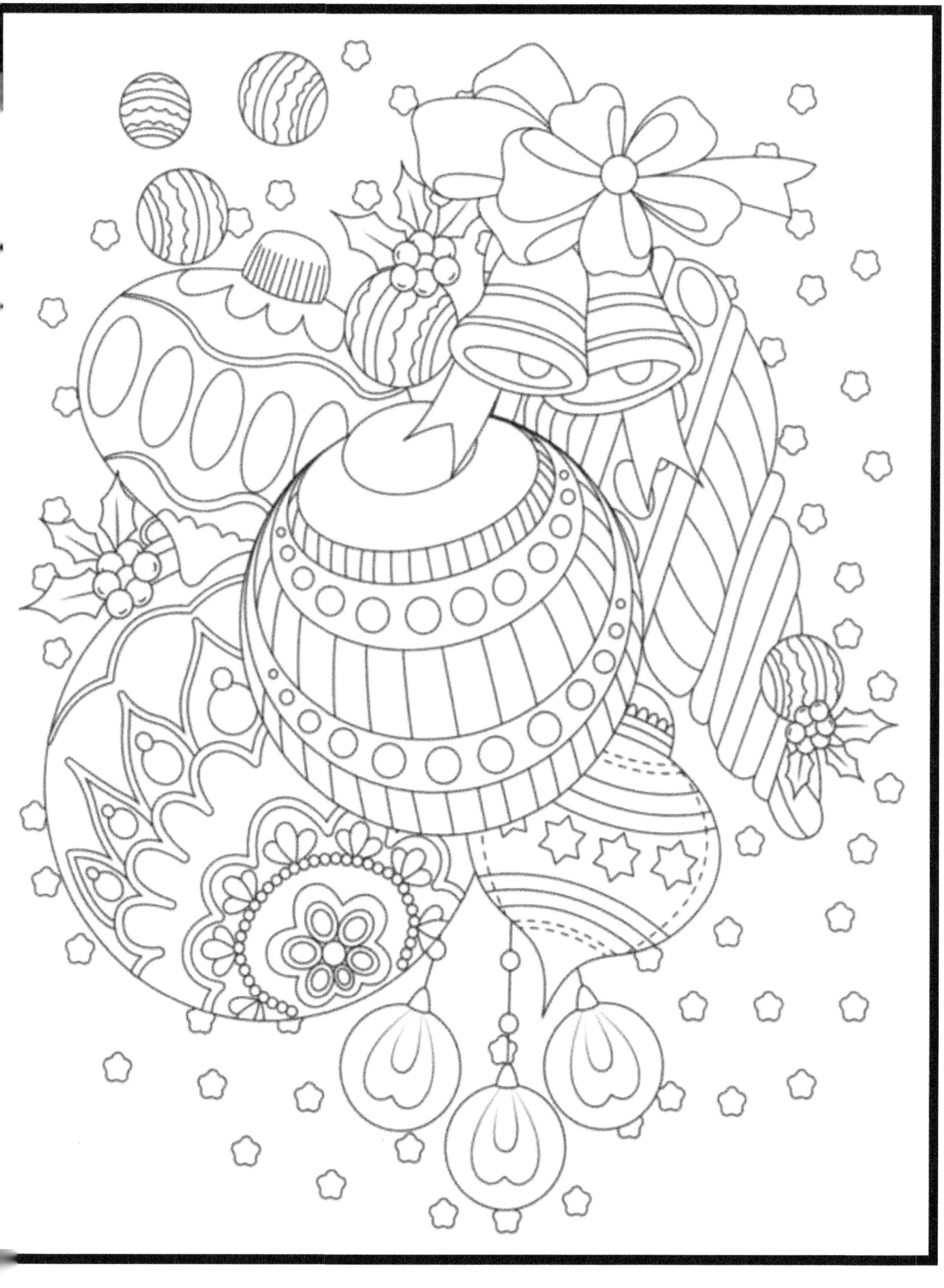

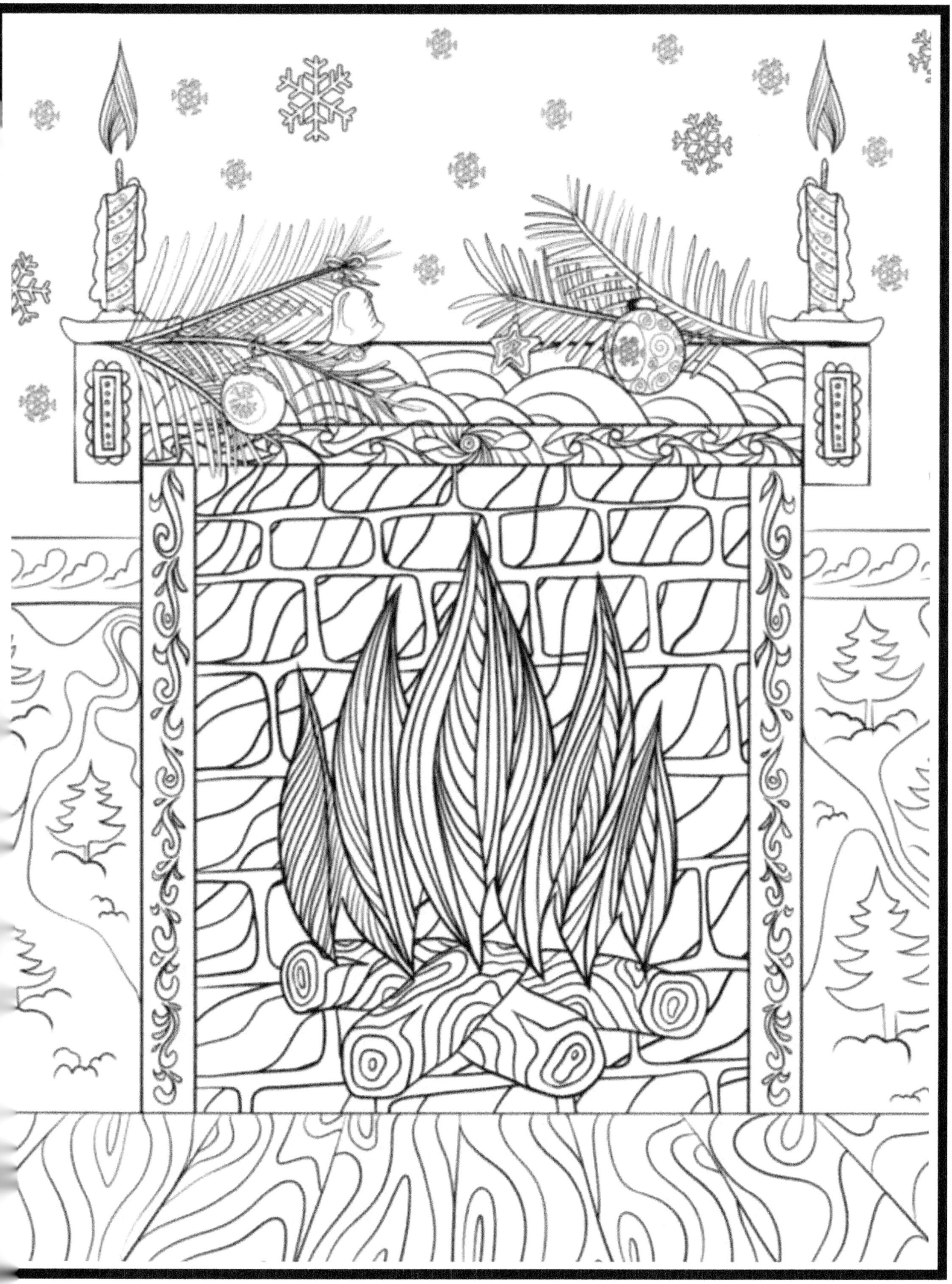

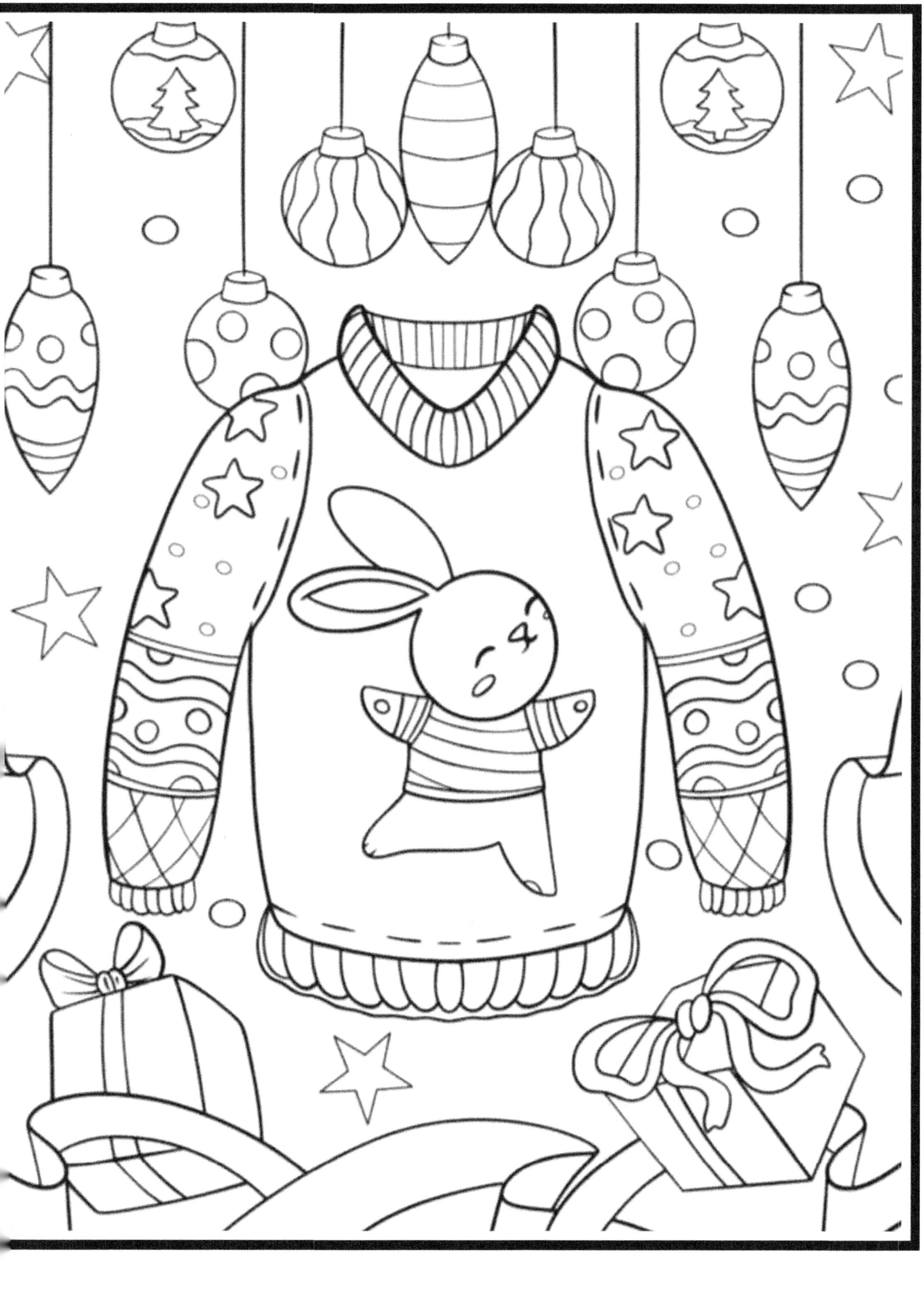

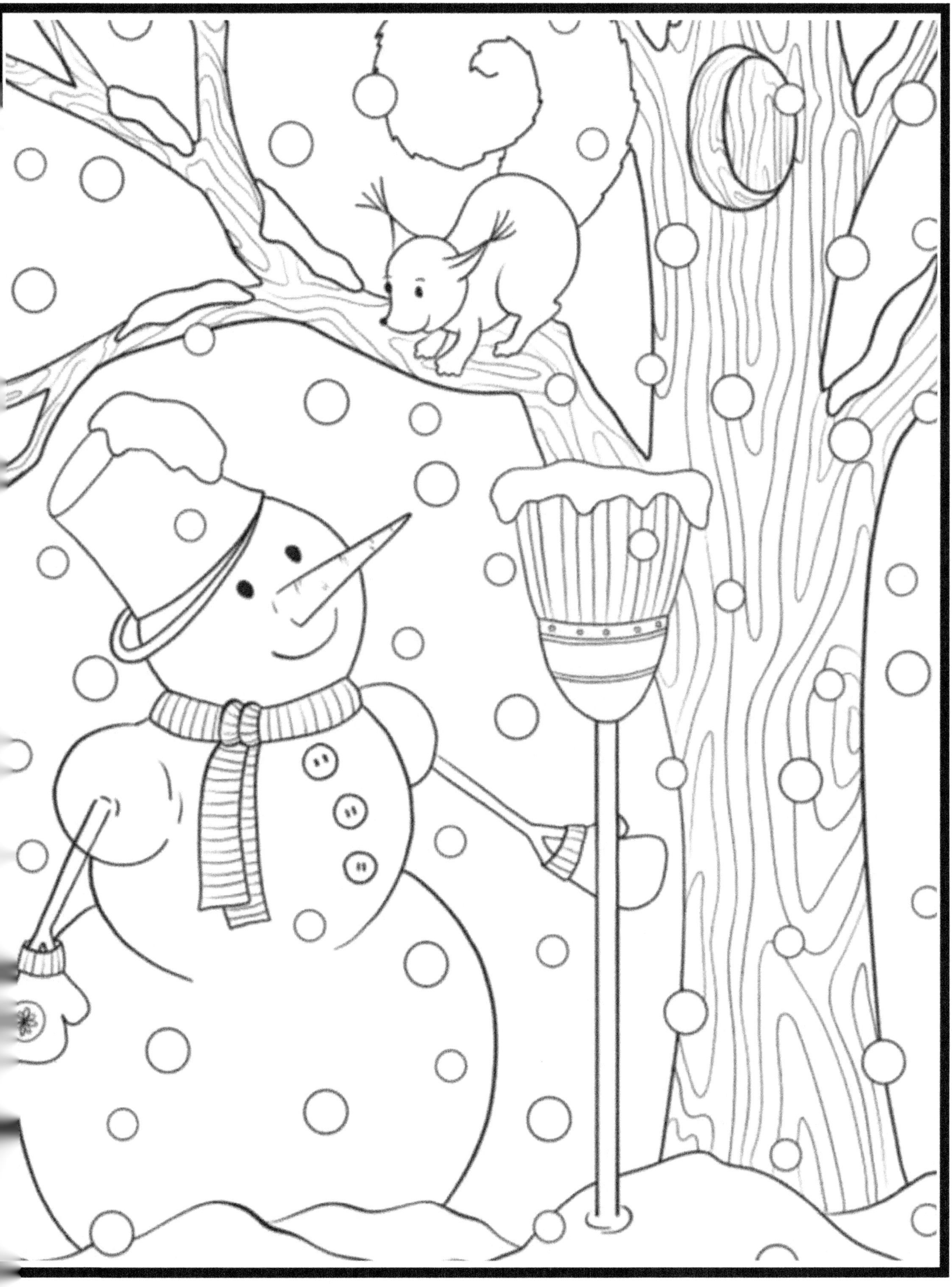

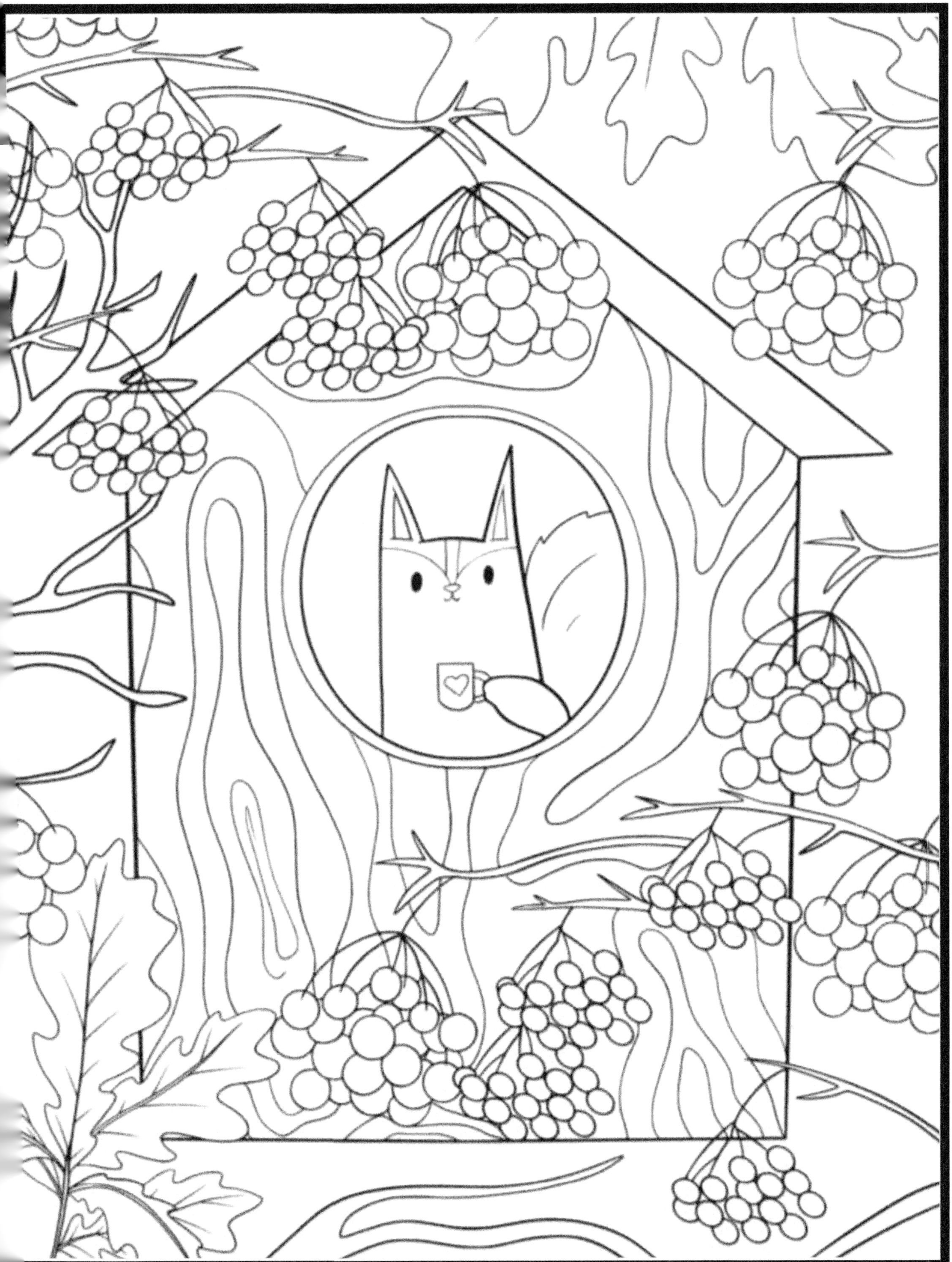

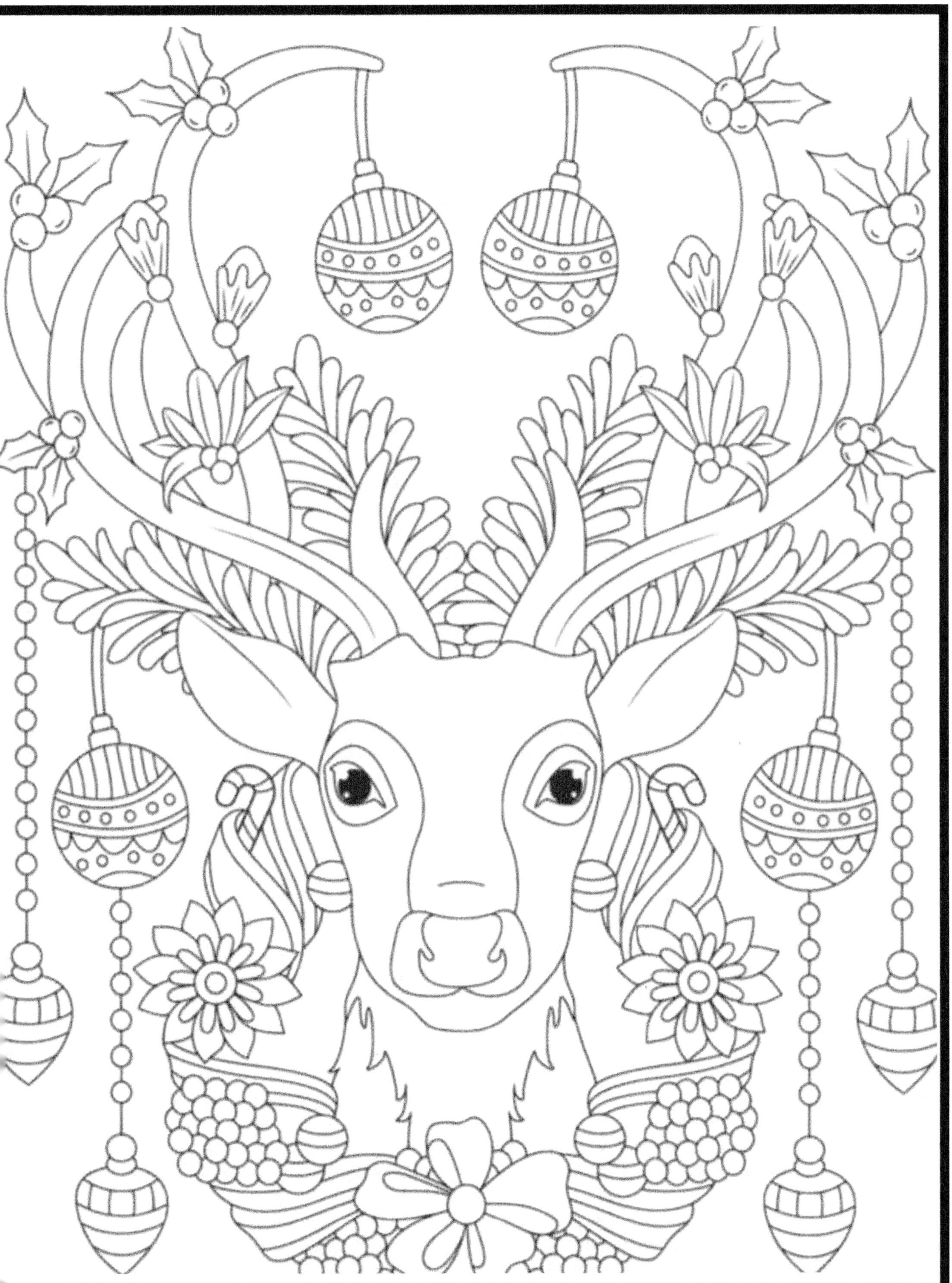

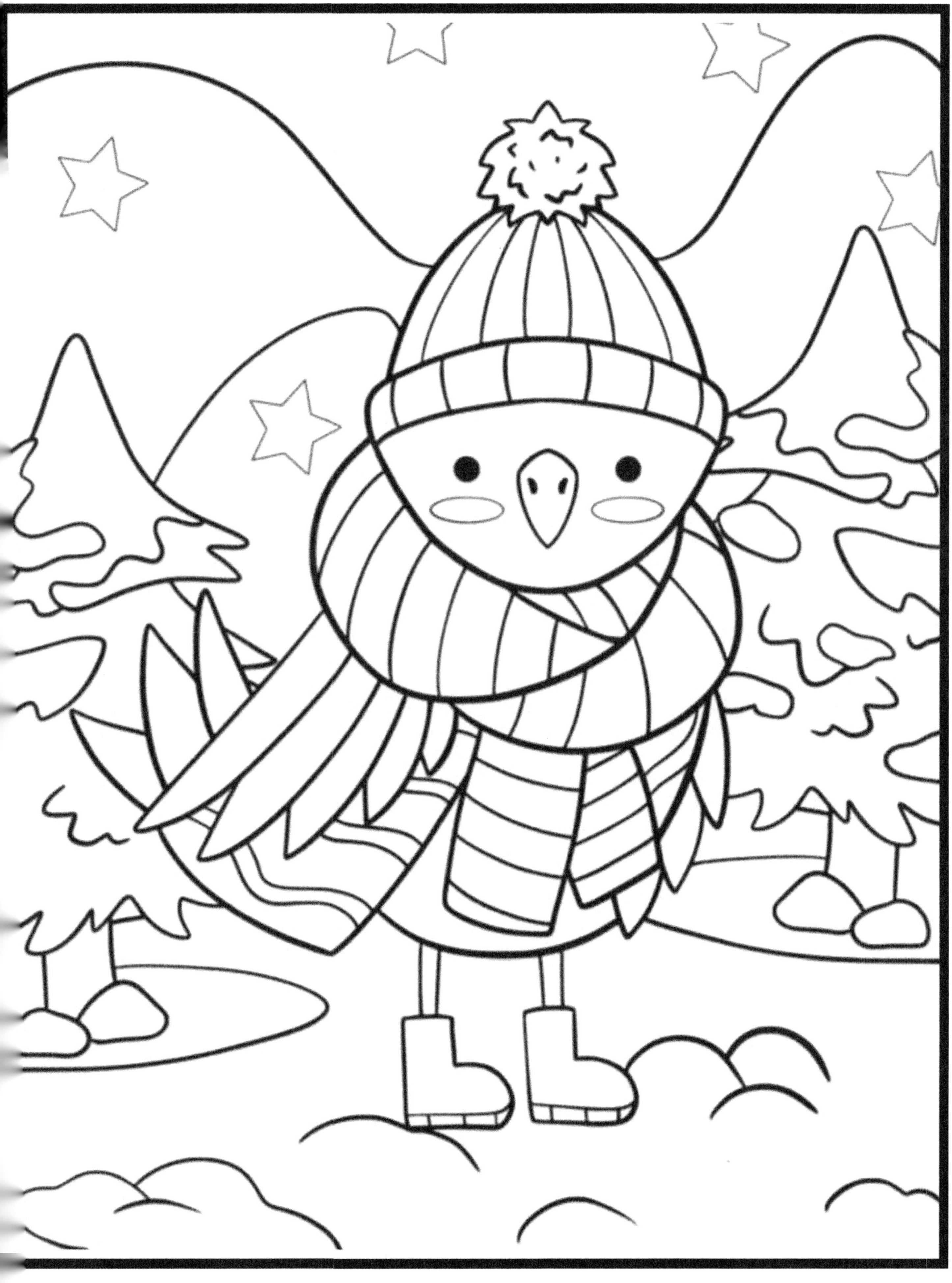

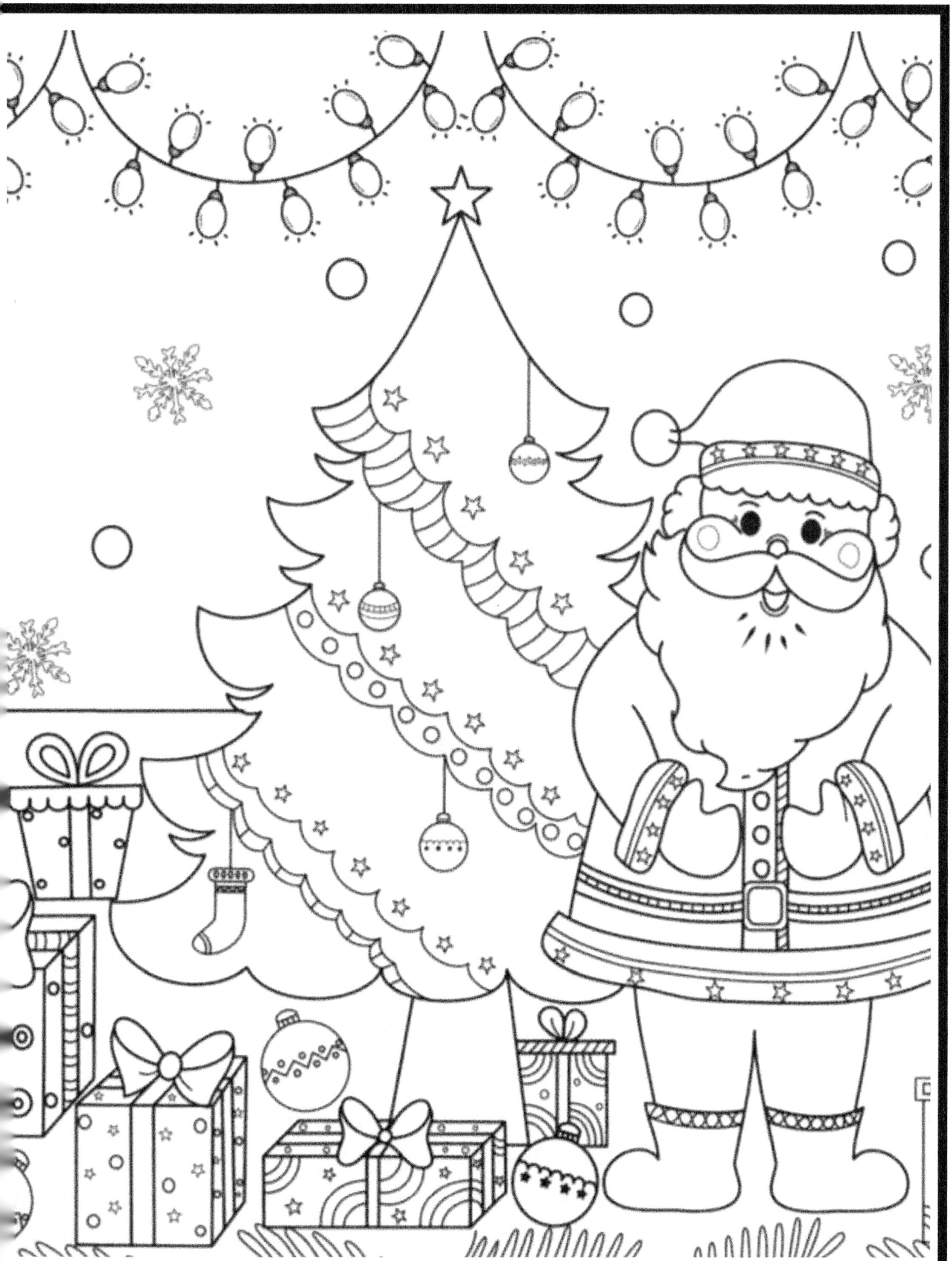

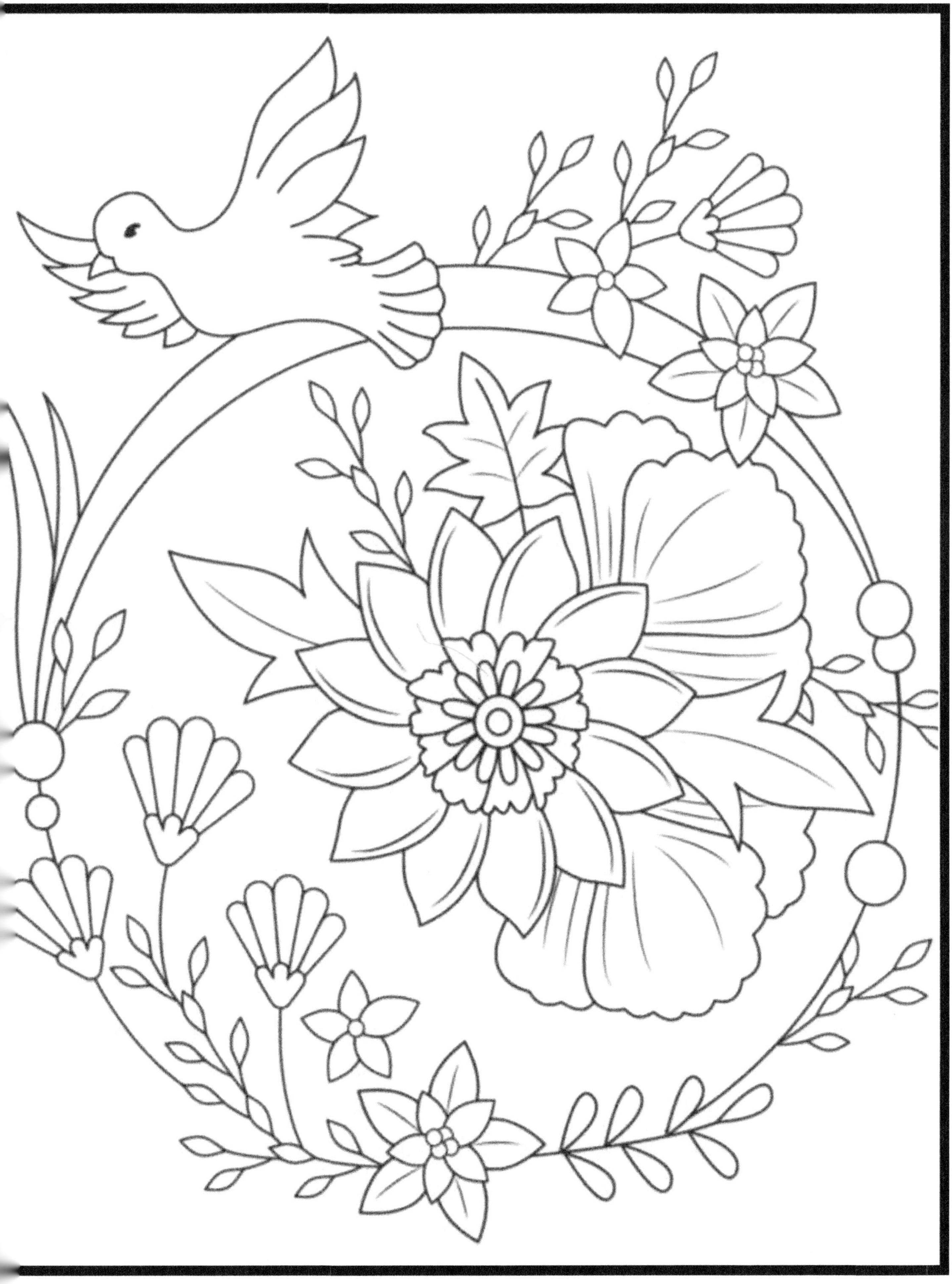

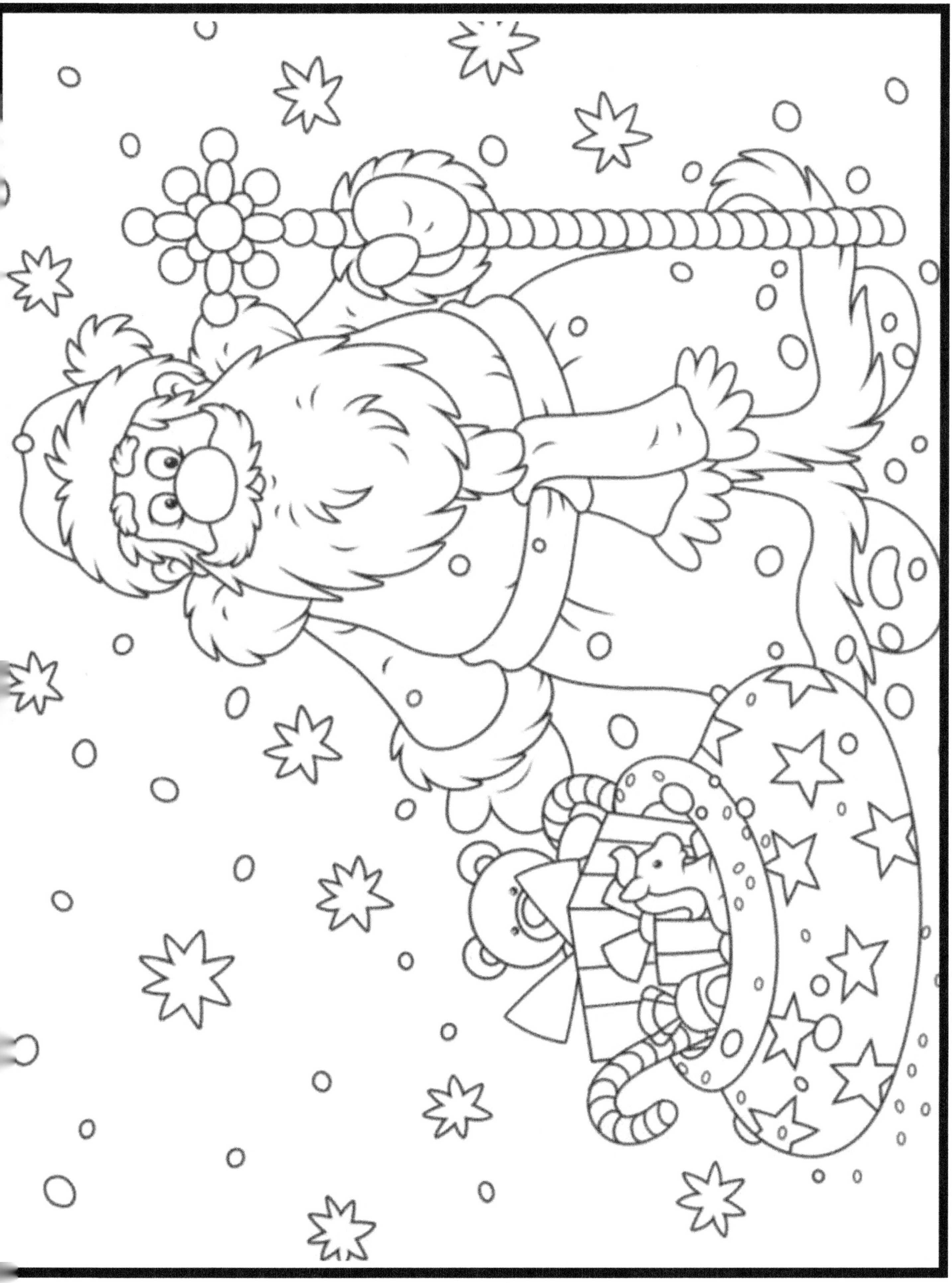

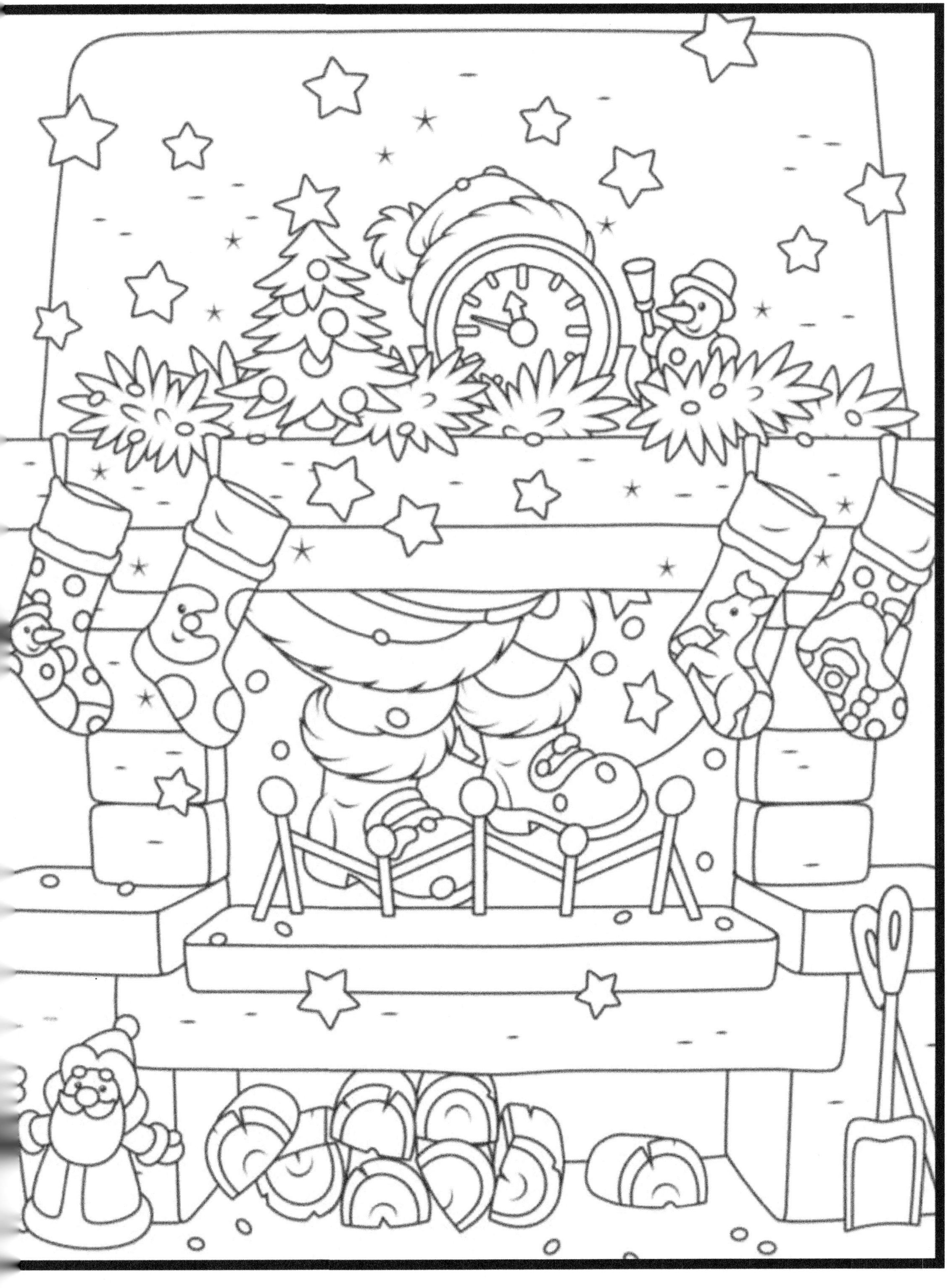

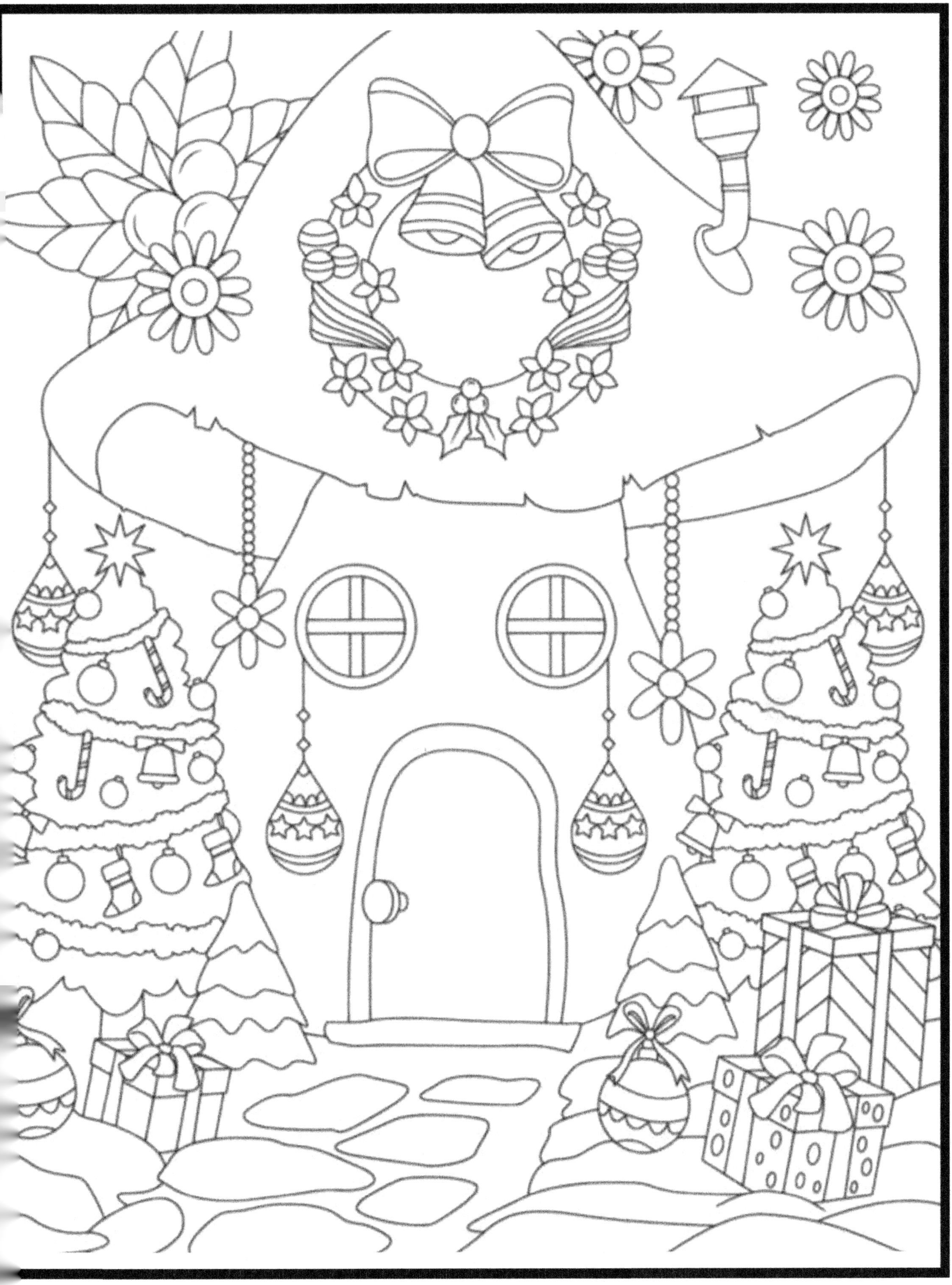

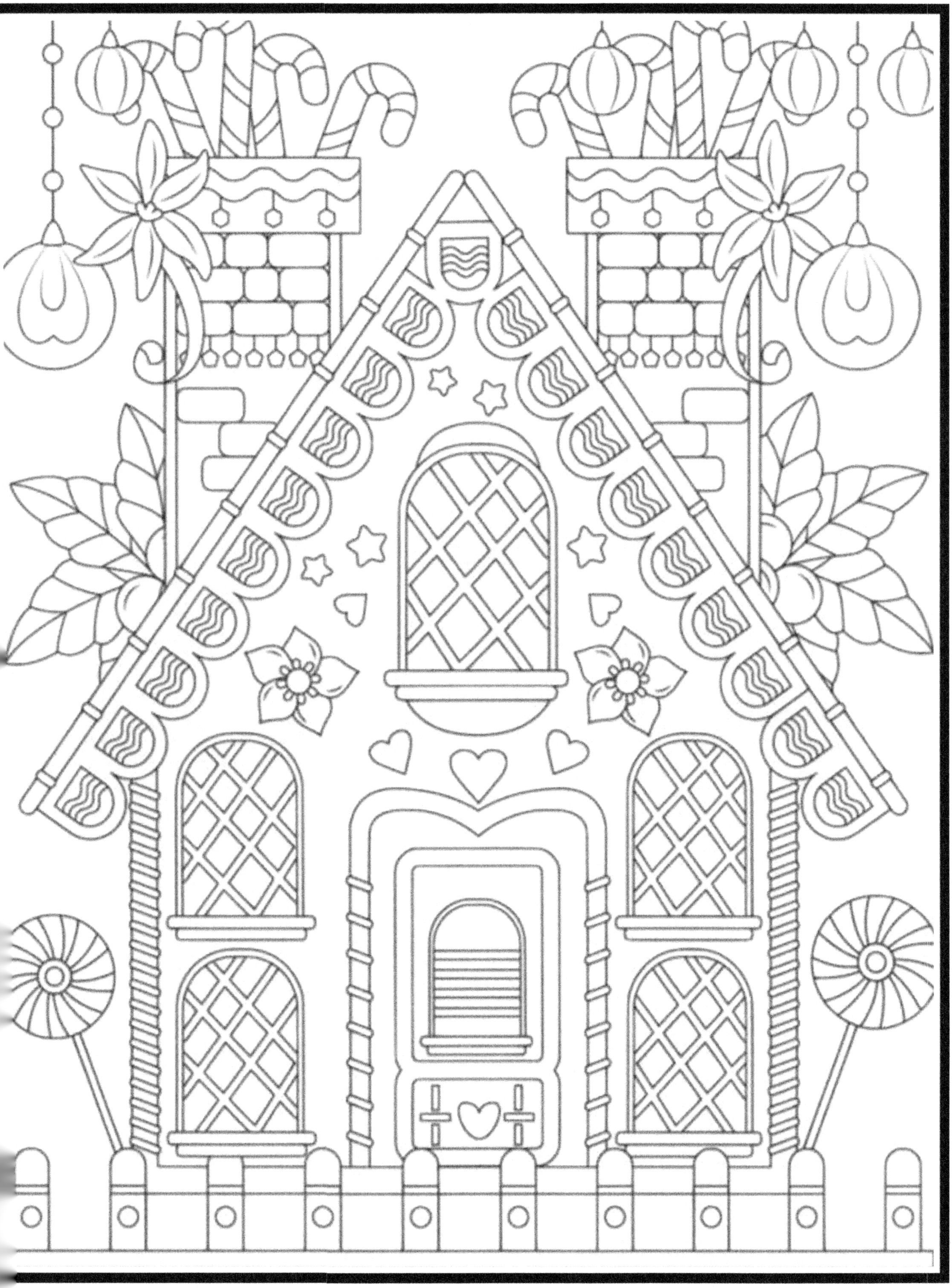

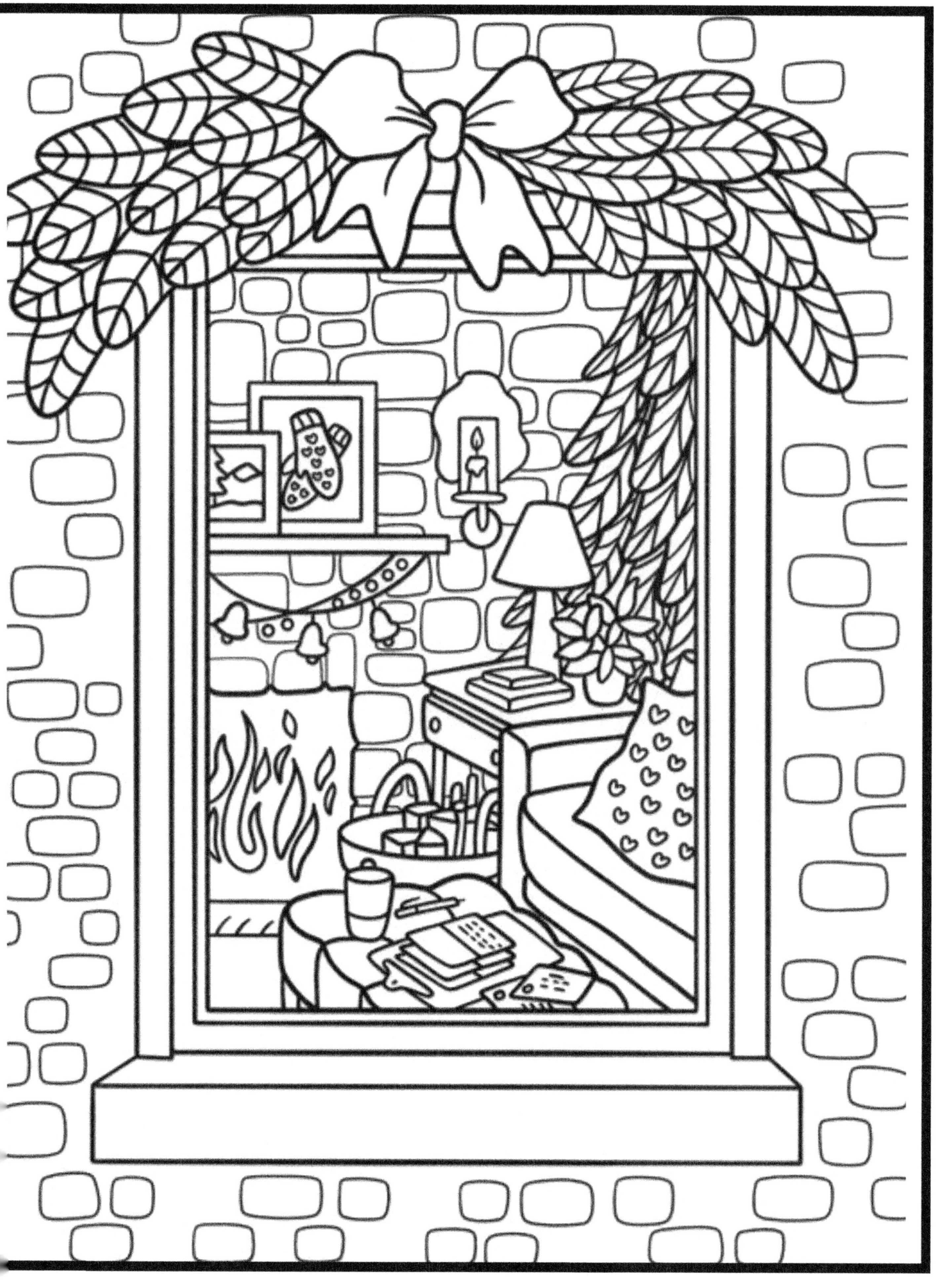

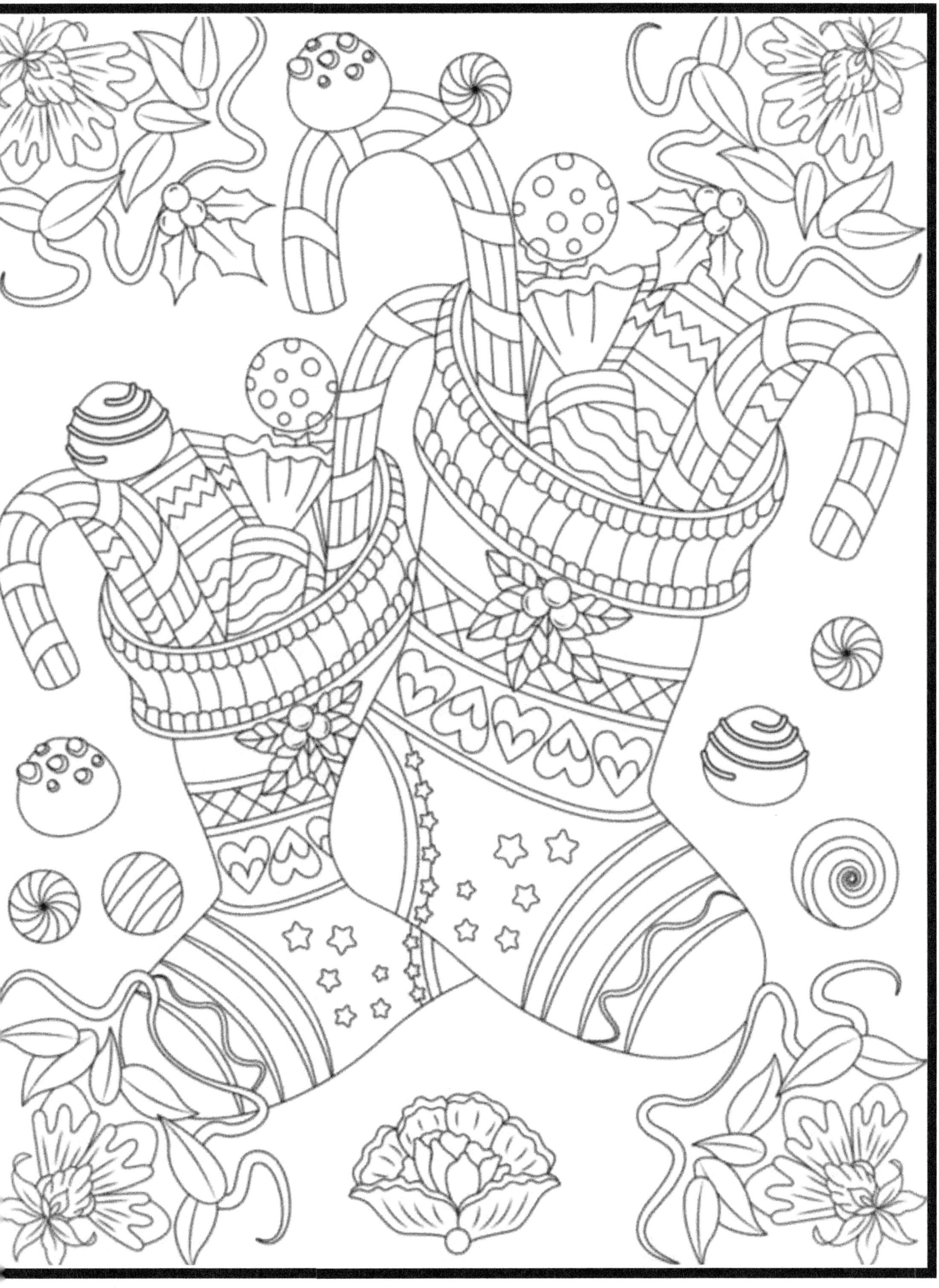

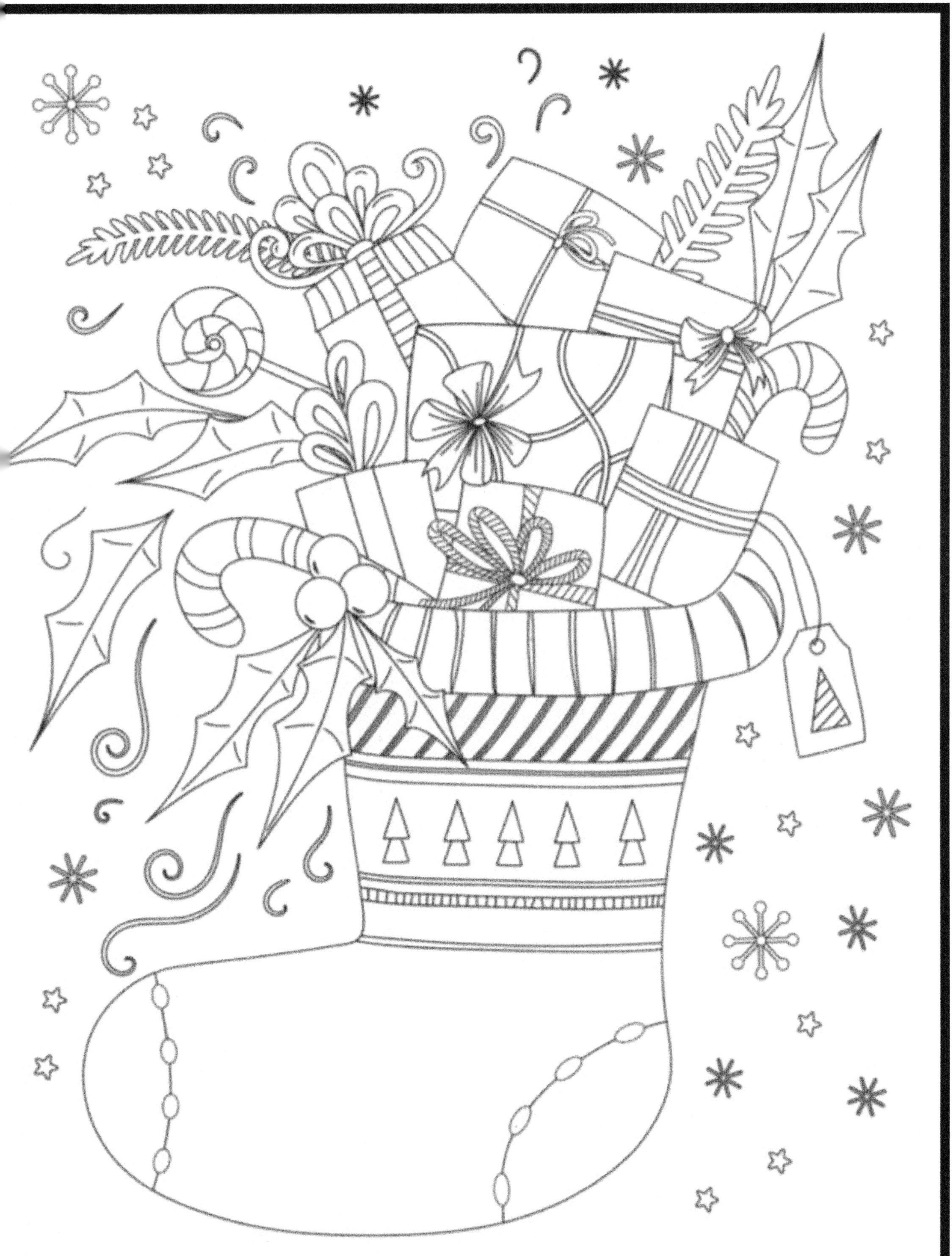

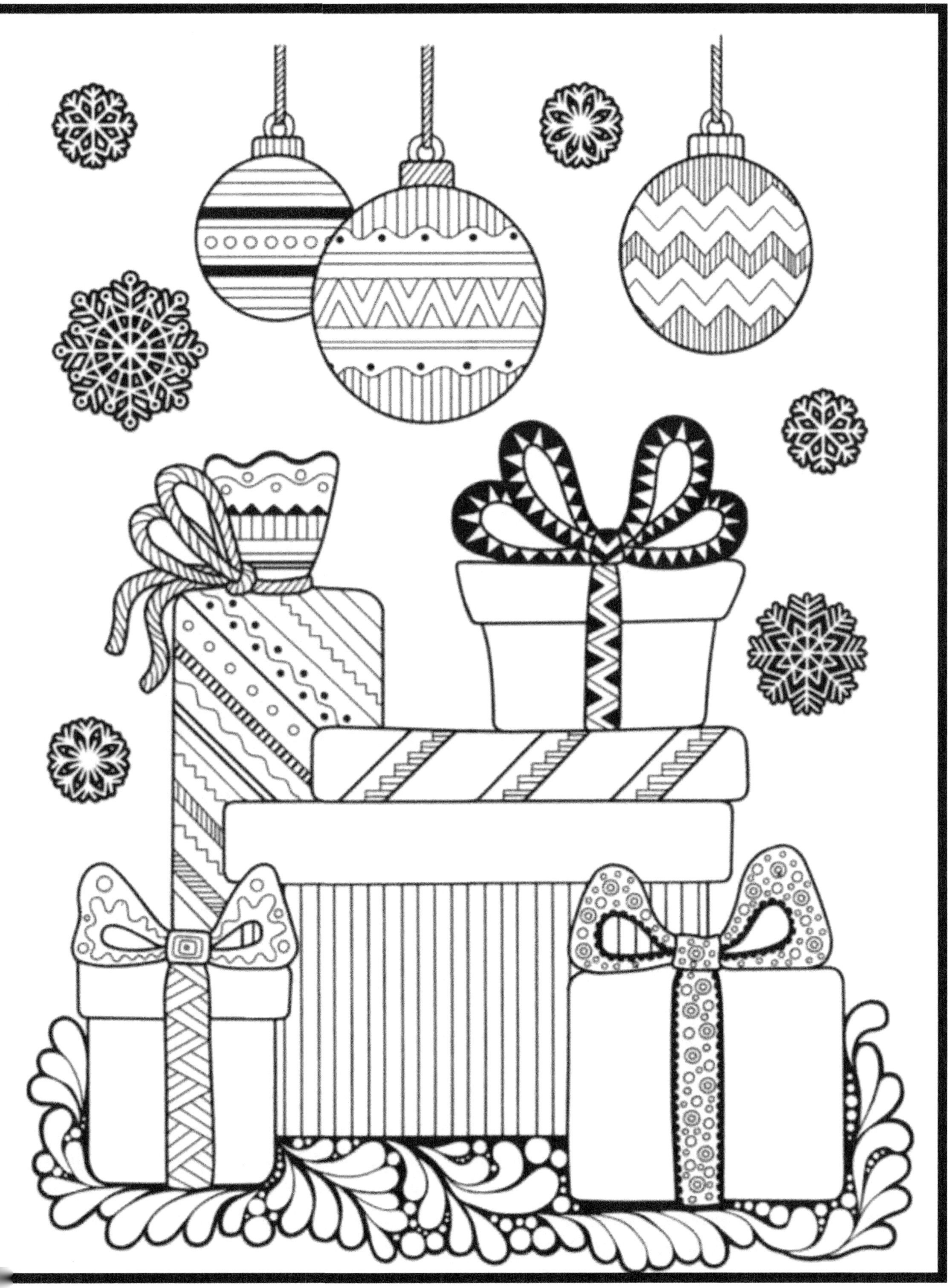

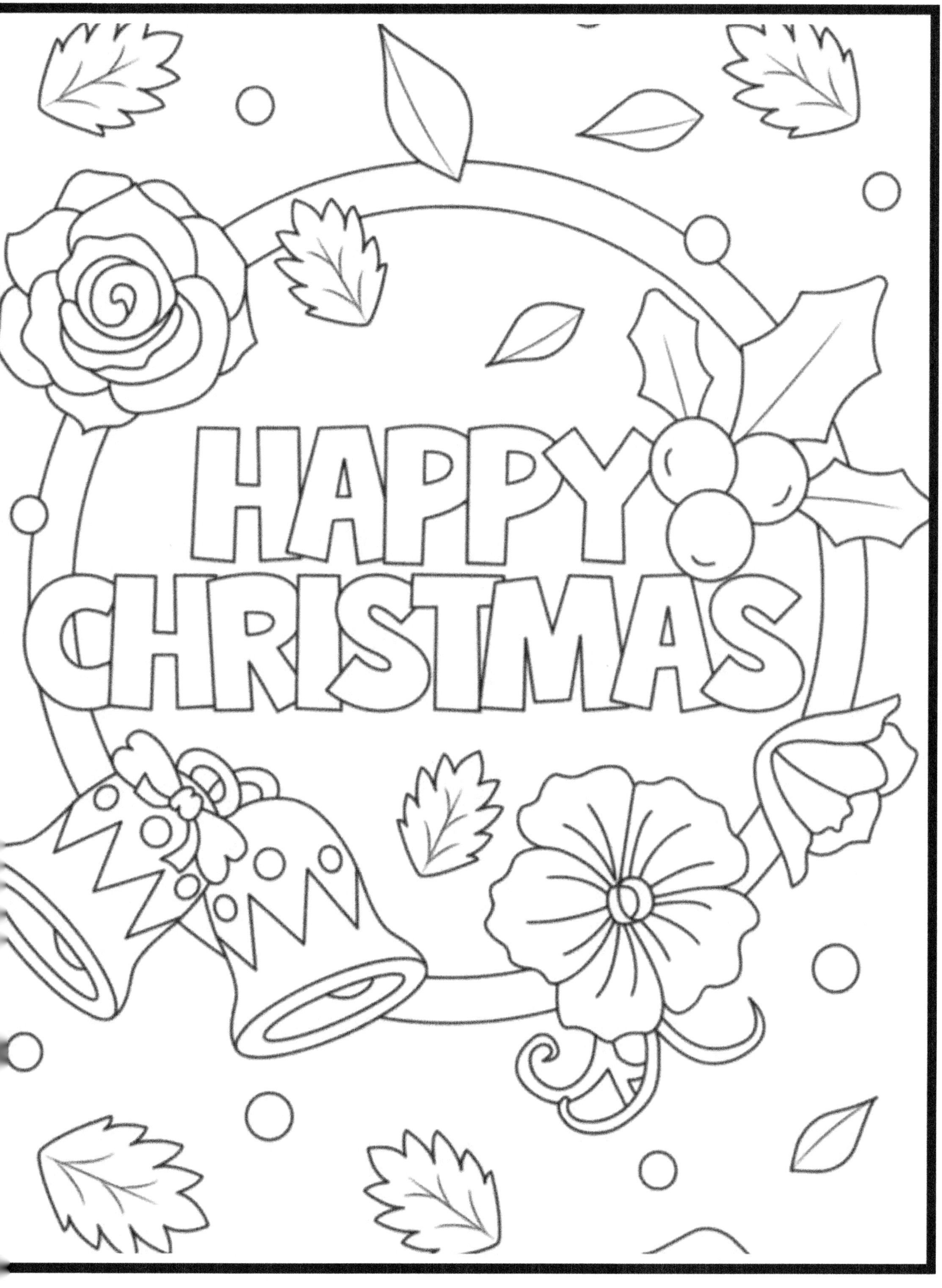
HAPPY
CHRISTMAS

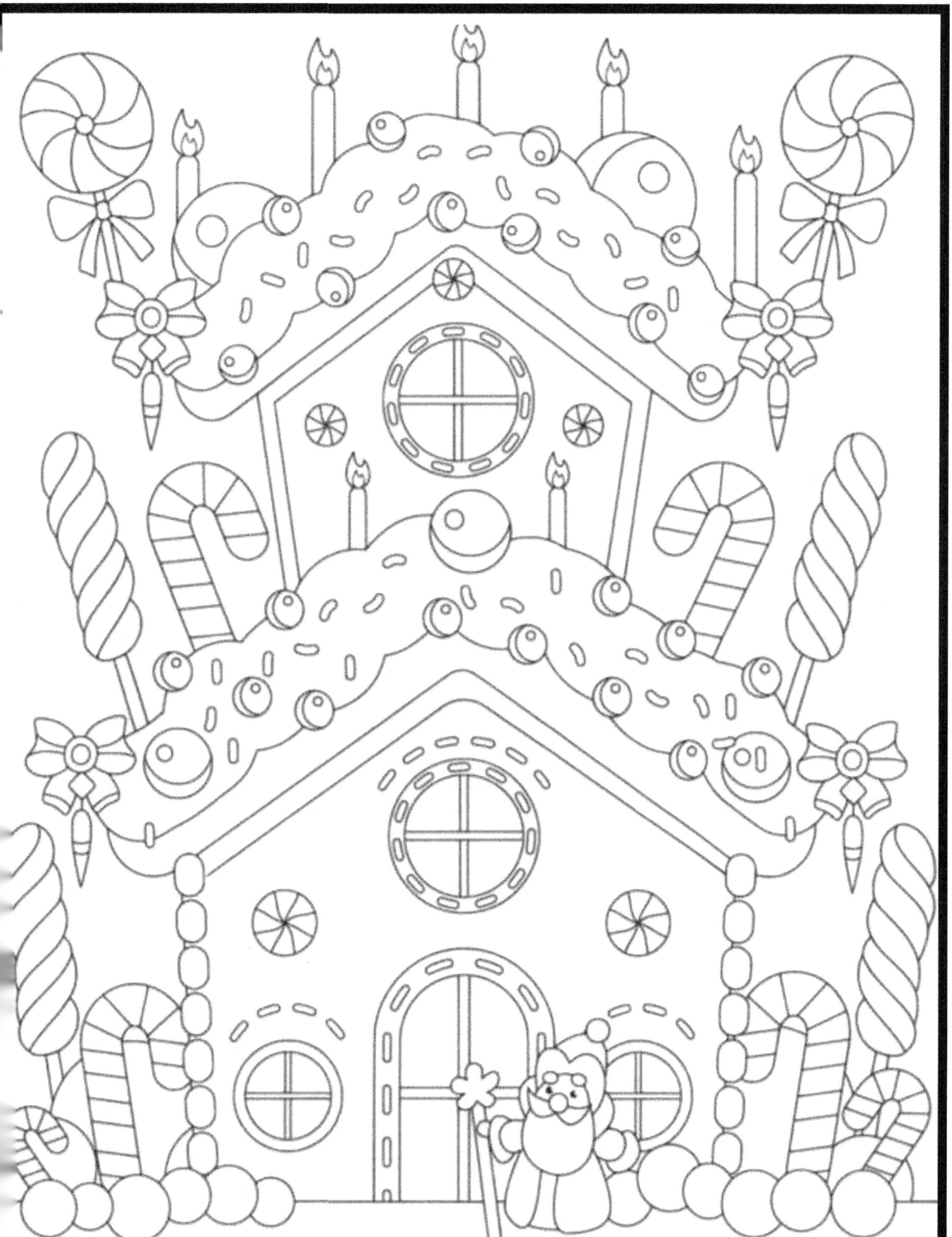

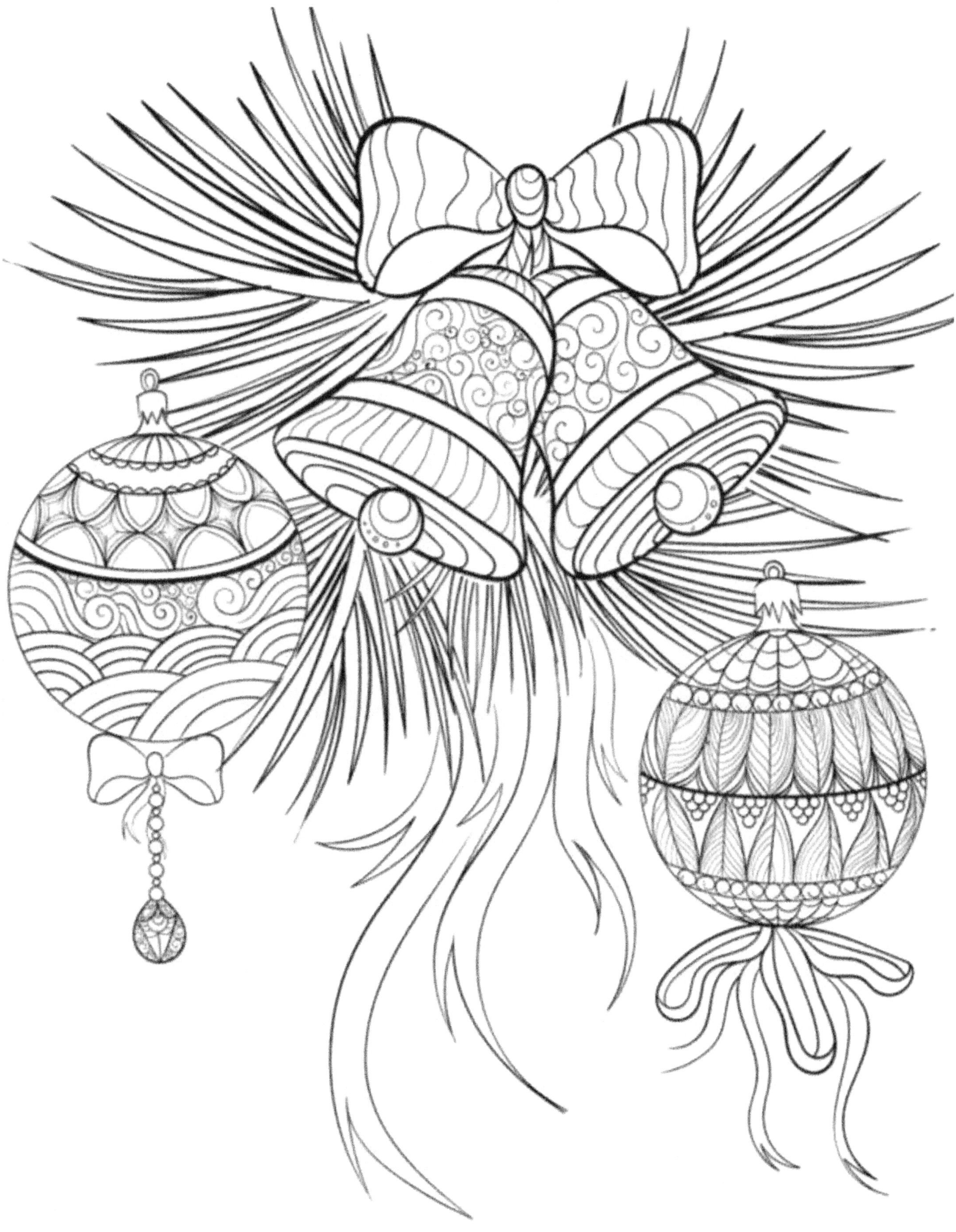

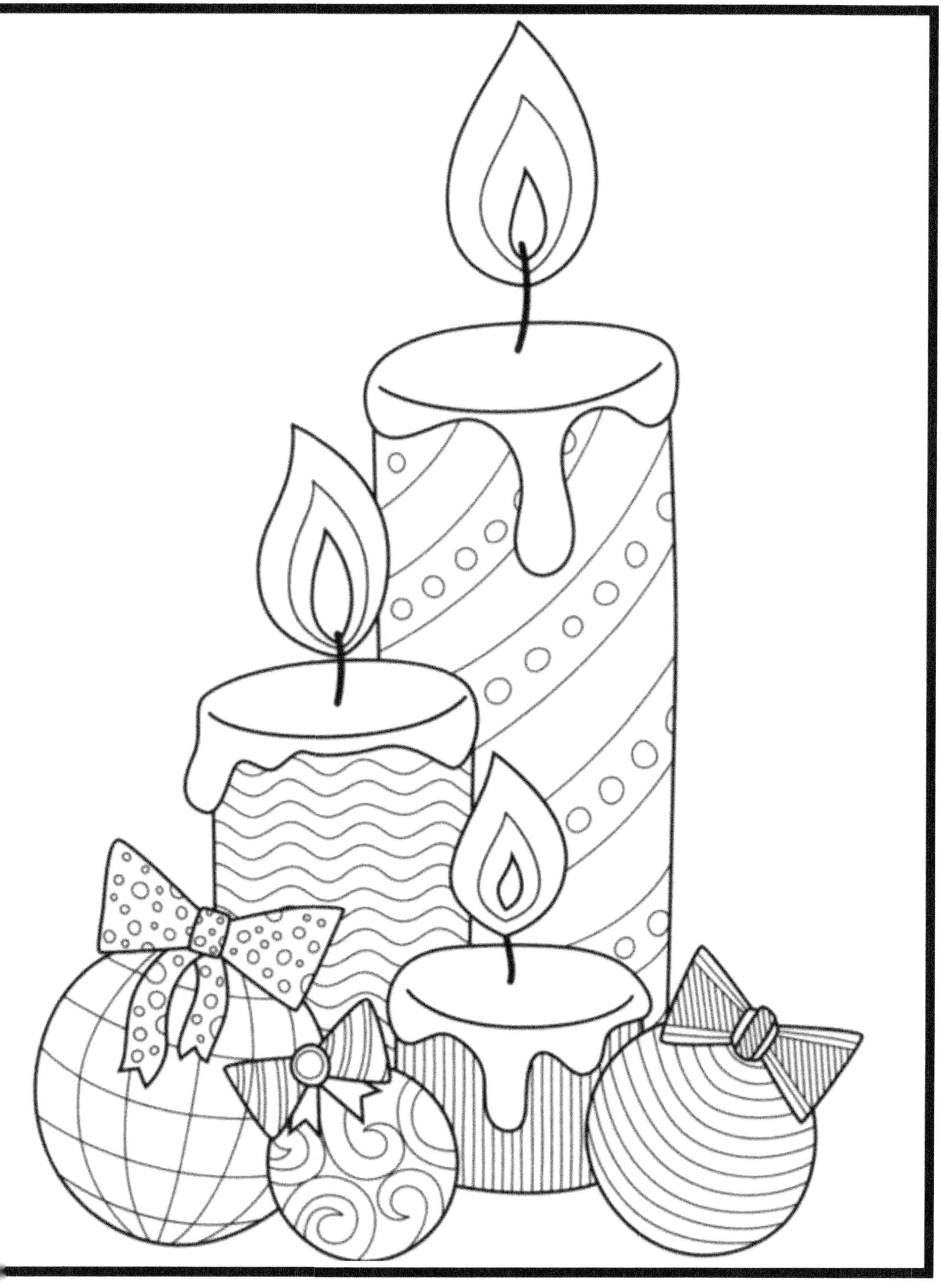

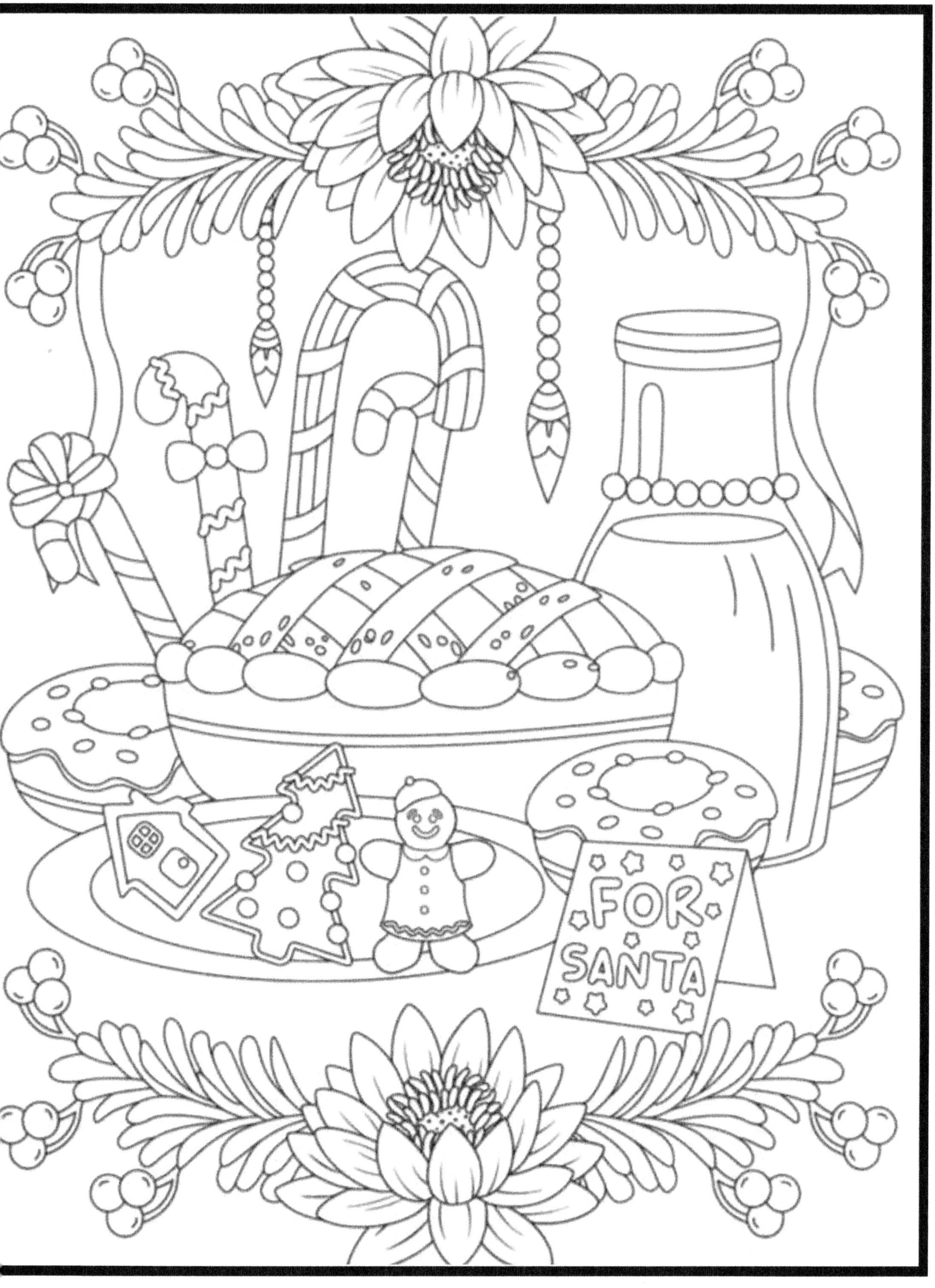
FOR
SANTA

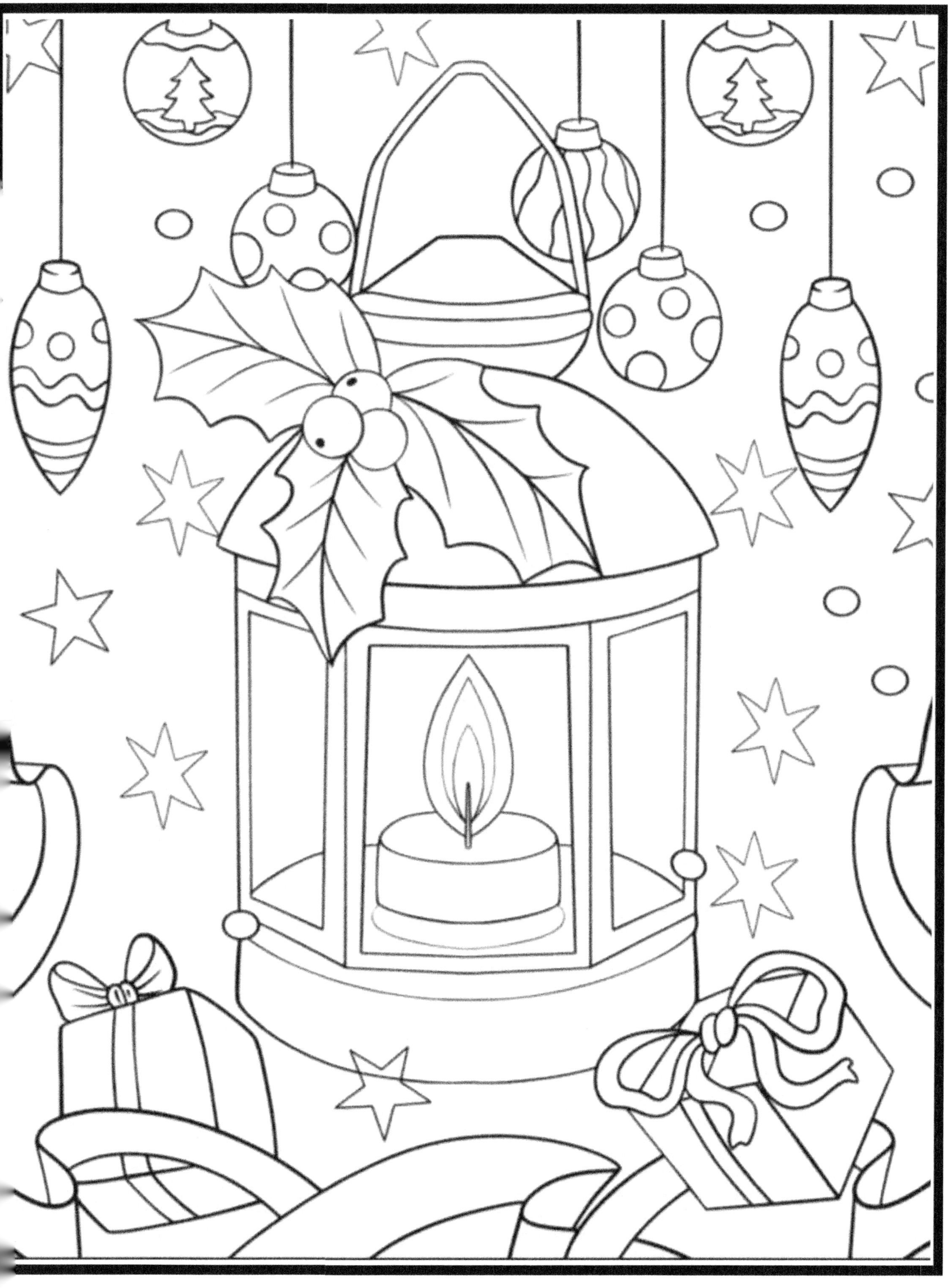

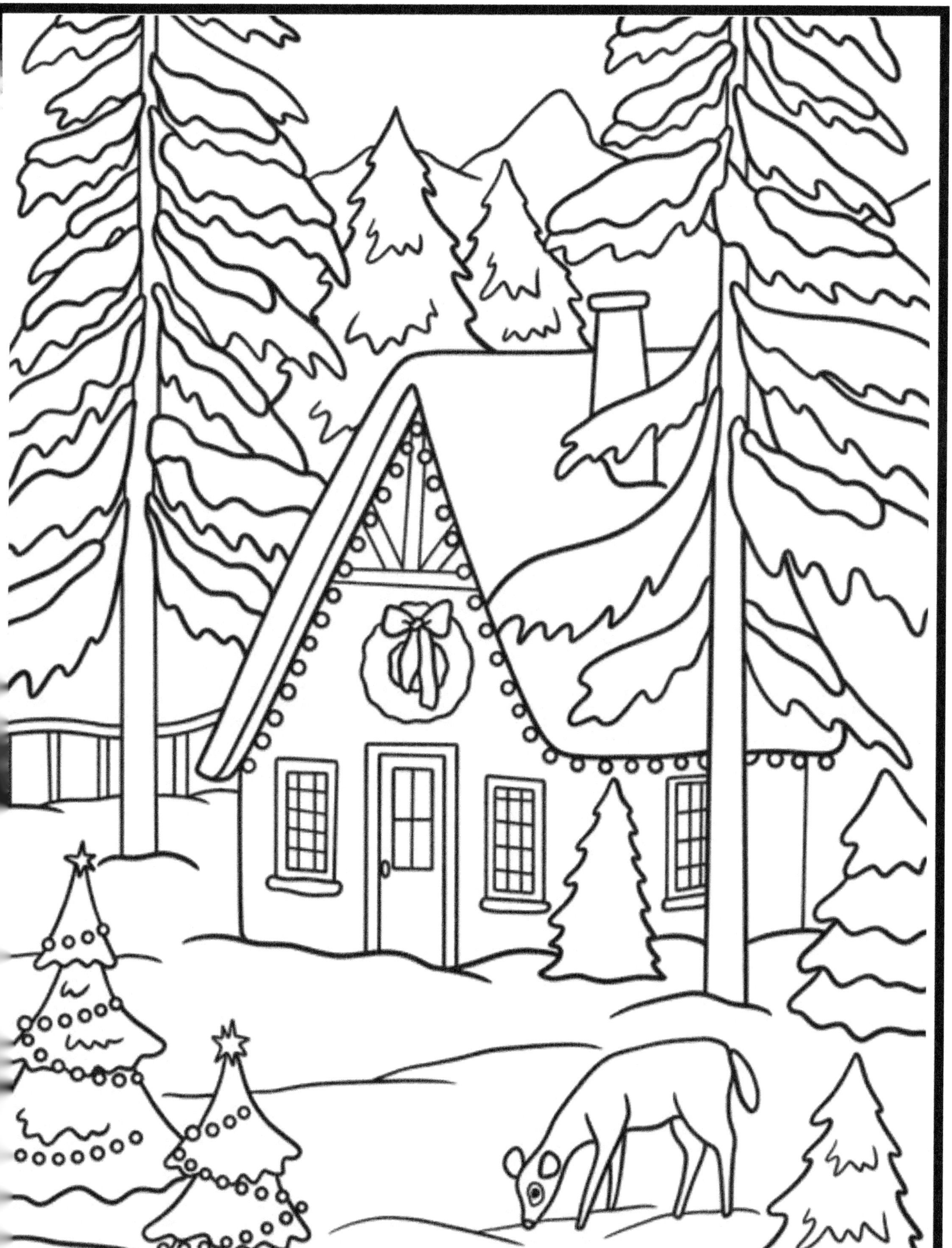

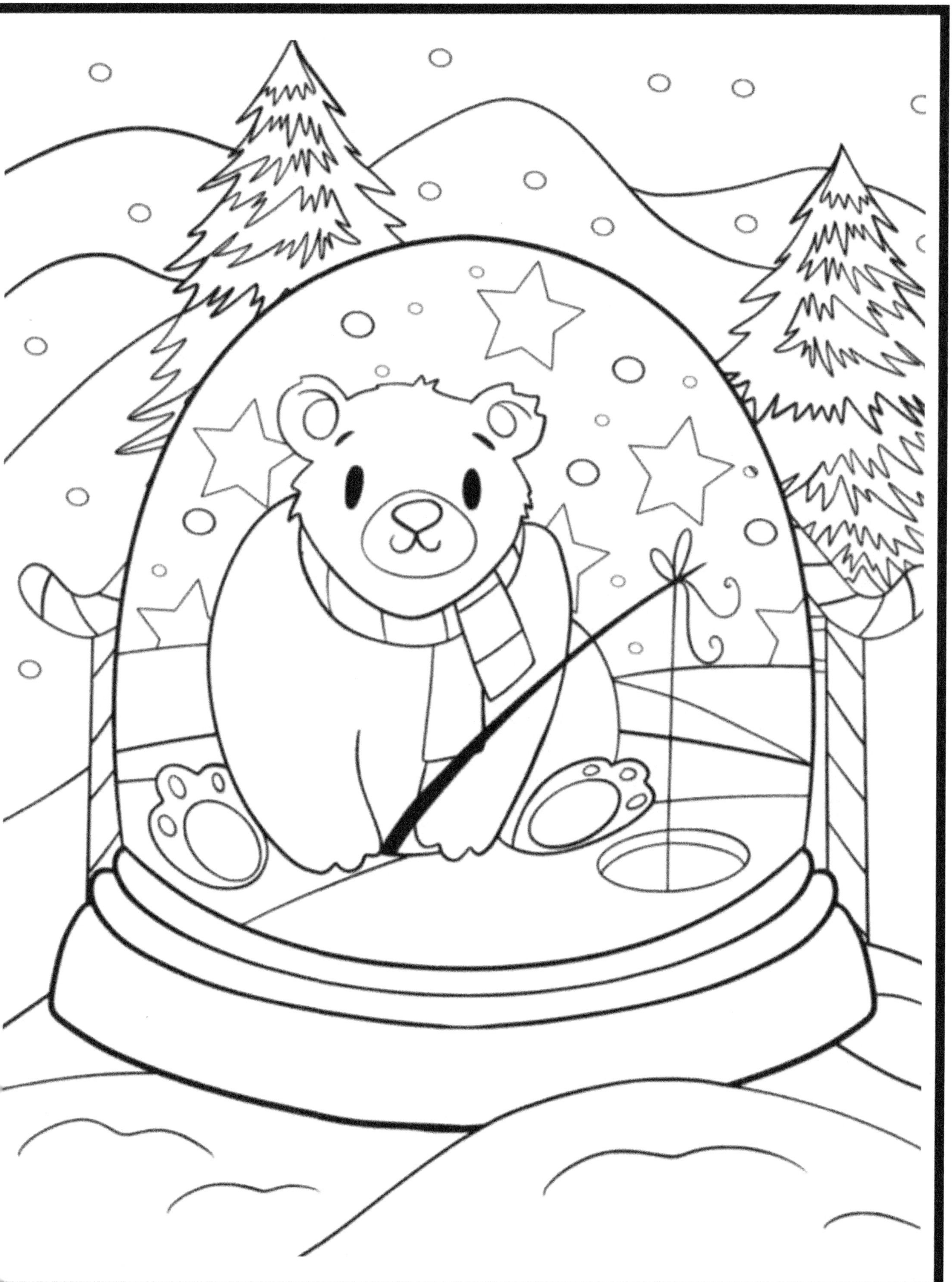

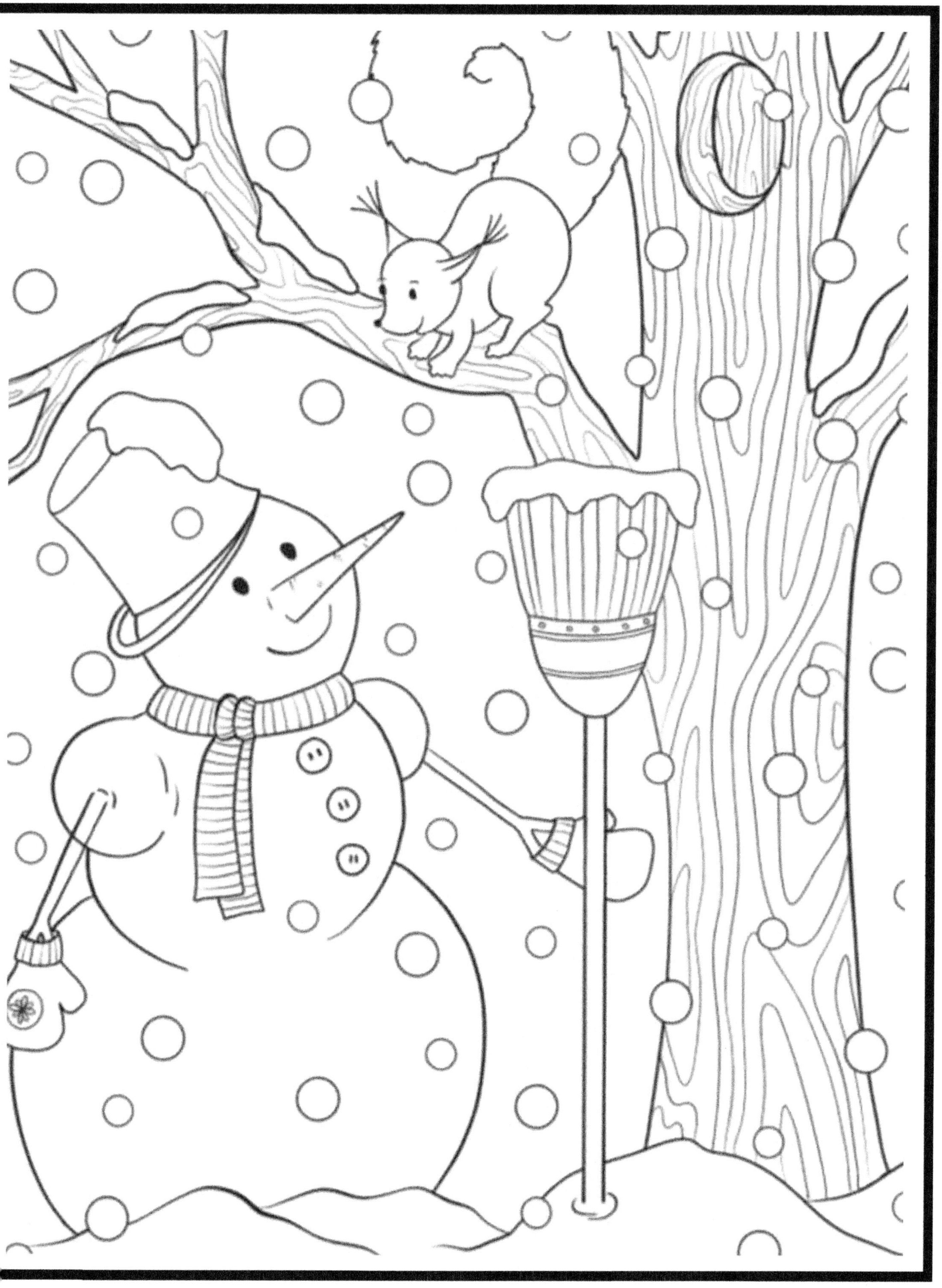